FRANCIS FRITH'S
TOWN & CITY
MEMORIES

RUGBY

SARAH PERNELL, originally a Londoner, has lived happily in Rugby since 1988. An author of historical fiction, she has a keen interest in both local and social history.

Rugby School 1922 72123

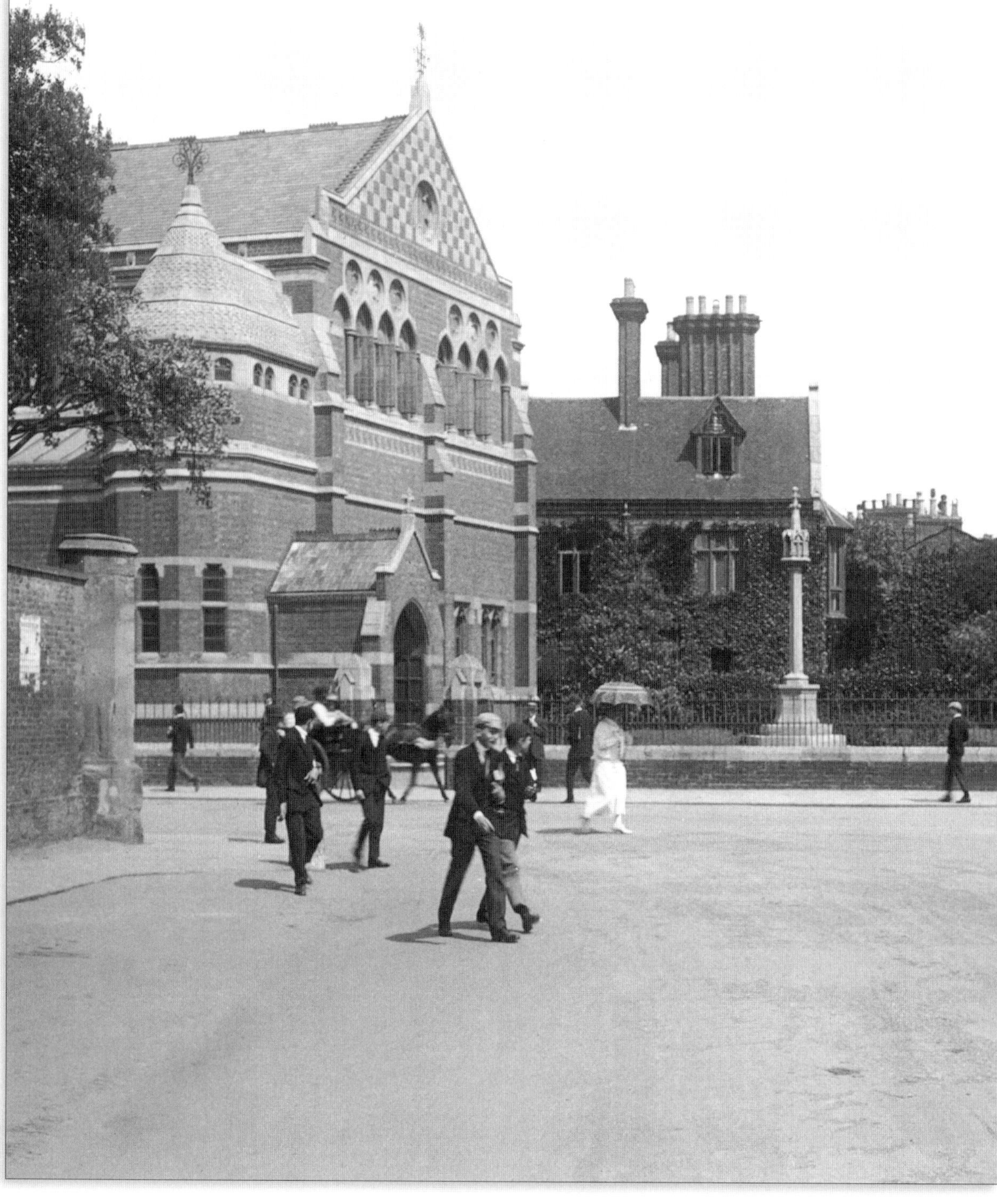

FRANCIS FRITH'S
TOWN & CITY
MEMORIES

RUGBY

SARAH PERNELL

FRANCIS FRITH'S
TOWN & CITY
MEMORIES

First published as Rugby, A Photographic History of your Town
in 2001 by Black Horse Books, an imprint of The Francis Frith Collection
Revised edition published in the United Kingdom in 2006 by
The Francis Frith Collection as Rugby, Town and City Memories
Limited Hardback Edition ISBN 1-84589-110-4
Paperback Edition ISBN 1-85937-620-7

British Library Cataloguing in Publication Data

Rugby
Town and City Memories
Sarah Pernell

The Francis Frith Collection®
Frith's Barn, Teffont,
Salisbury, Wiltshire SP3 5QP
Tel: +44 (0) 1722 716 376
Email: info@francisfrith.co.uk
www.francisfrith.com

Aerial photographs reproduced under licence from Simmons Aerofilms Limited
Historical Ordnance Survey maps reproduced under licence from Homecheck.co.uk

Printed and bound in England

Front Cover: **RUGBY, MARKET PLACE 1932** 85177t
The colour-tinting in this image is for illustrative purposes only,
and is not intended to be historically accurate

Every attempt has been made to contact copyright holders of illustrative material.
We will be happy to give full acknowledgement in future editions for any items not credited.
Any information should be directed to The Francis Frith Collection.

AS WITH ANY HISTORICAL DATABASE, THE FRANCIS FRITH ARCHIVE IS CONSTANTLY BEING CORRECTED AND IMPROVED, AND THE PUBLISHERS WOULD WELCOME INFORMATION ON OMISSIONS OR INACCURACIES

FRANCIS FRITH'S

TOWN & CITY

MEMORIES

CONTENTS

THE MAKING OF AN ARCHIVE

Francis Frith, Victorian founder of the world-famous photographic archive, was a devout Quaker and a highly successful Victorian businessman. By 1860 he was already a multi-millionaire, having established and sold a wholesale grocery business in Liverpool. He had also made a series of pioneering photographic journeys to the Nile region. The images he returned with were the talk of London. An eminent modern historian has likened their impact on the population of the time to that on our own generation of the first photographs taken on the surface of the moon.

Frith had a passion for landscape, and was as equally inspired by the countryside of Britain as he was by the desert regions of the Nile. He resolved to set out on a new career and to use his skills with a camera. He established a business in Reigate as a specialist publisher of topographical photographs.

Frith lived in an era of immense and sometimes violent change. For the poor in the early part of Victoria's reign work was a drudge and the hours long, and ordinary people had precious little free time. Most had not travelled far beyond the boundaries of their own town or village. Mass tourism was in its infancy during the 1860s, but during the next decade the railway network and the establishment of Bank Holidays and half-Saturdays gradually made it possible for the working man and his family to enjoy holidays and to see a little more of the world. With characteristic business acumen, Francis Frith foresaw that these new tourists would enjoy having souvenirs to commemorate their days out. He began selling photo-souvenirs of seaside resorts and beauty spots, which the Victorian public pasted into treasured family albums.

Frith's aim was to photograph every town and village in Britain. For the next thirty years he travelled the country by train and by pony and trap, producing fine photographs of seaside resorts and beauty spots that were keenly bought by millions of Victorians.

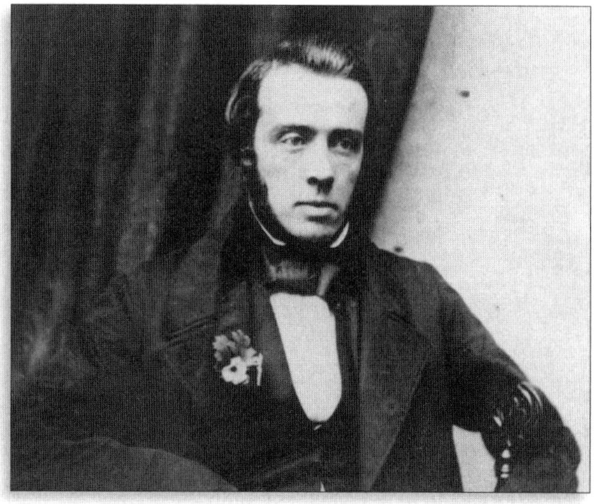

THE RISE OF FRITH & CO

Each photograph was taken with tourism in mind, the small team of Frith photographers concentrating on busy shopping streets, beaches, seafronts, picturesque lanes and villages. They also photographed buildings: the Victorian and Edwardian eras were times of huge building activity, and town halls, libraries, post offices, schools and technical colleges were springing up all over the country. They were invariably celebrated by a proud Victorian public, and photo souvenirs – visual records – published by F Frith & Co were sold in their hundreds of thousands. In addition, many new commercial buildings such as hotels, inns and pubs were photographed, often because their owners specifically commissioned Frith postcards or prints of them for re-sale or for publicity purposes.

In order to gain some understanding of the scale of Frith's business one only has to look at the catalogue issued by Frith & Co in 1886: it runs to some 670 pages. By 1890 Frith had created the greatest specialist photographic publishing company in the world, with over 2,000 stockists! The picture on the right shows the Frith & Co display board on the wall of the stockist at Ingleton in the Yorkshire Dales (left of window). Beautifully constructed with a mahogany frame and gilt inserts, it displayed a dozen scenes.

POSTCARD BONANZA

The ever-popular holiday postcard we know today took many years to appear, and F Frith & Co was in the vanguard of its development. Postcards became a hugely popular means of communication and sold in their millions. Frith's company took full advantage of this boom and soon became the major publisher of photographic view postcards.

Francis Frith died in 1898 at his villa in Cannes, his great project still growing. His sons Eustace and Cyril continued their father's monumental task, expanding the number of views offered to the public and recording more and more places in Britain, as the coasts and countryside were opened up to mass travel. The archive Frith created continued in business for another seventy years. By 1970 it contained over a third of a million pictures of 7,000 cities, towns and villages. The massive photographic record Frith has left to us stands as a living monument to a special and very remarkable man.

This book shows Rugby as it was photographed by this world-famous archive at various periods in its development over the past 150 years. Every photograph was taken for a specific commercial purpose, which explains why the selection may not show every aspect of the town landscape. However, the photographs, compiled from one of the world's most celebrated archives, provide an important and absorbing record of your town.

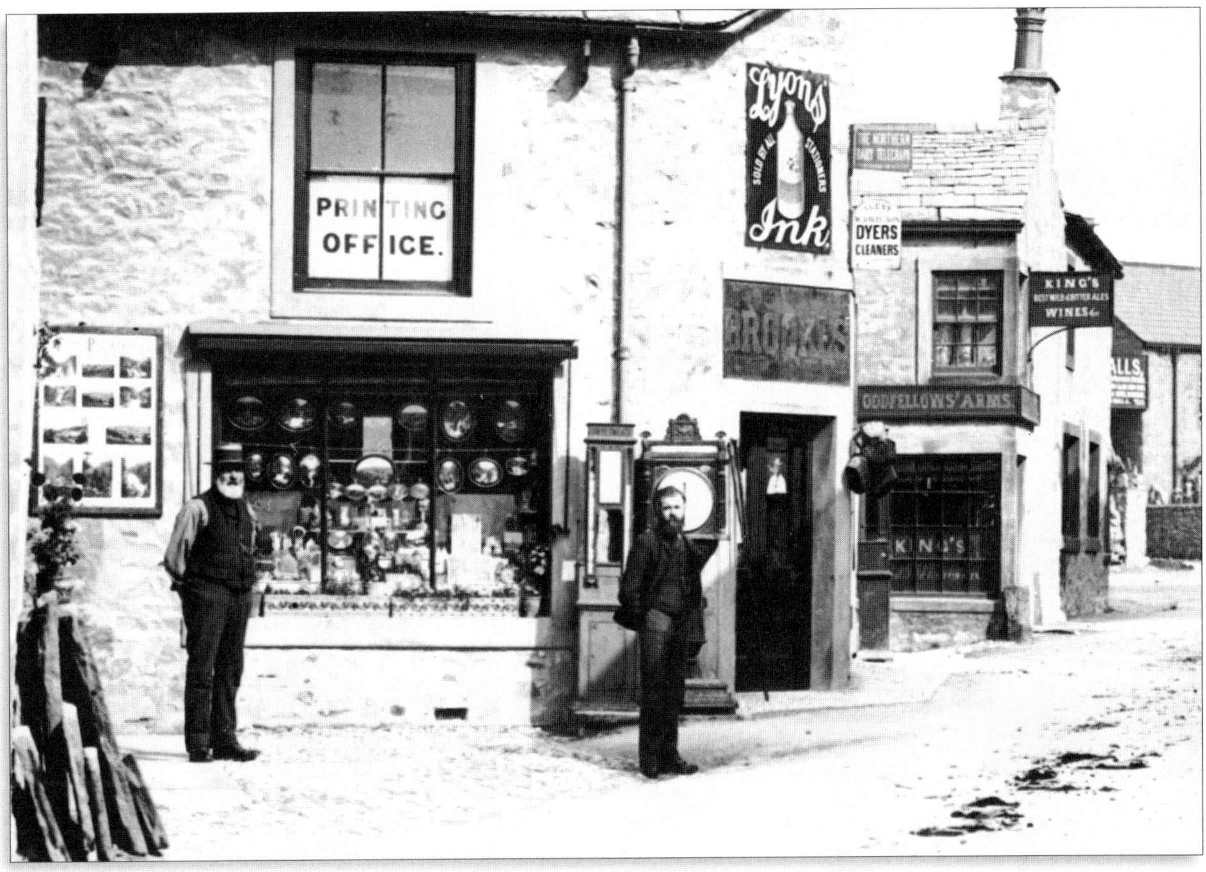

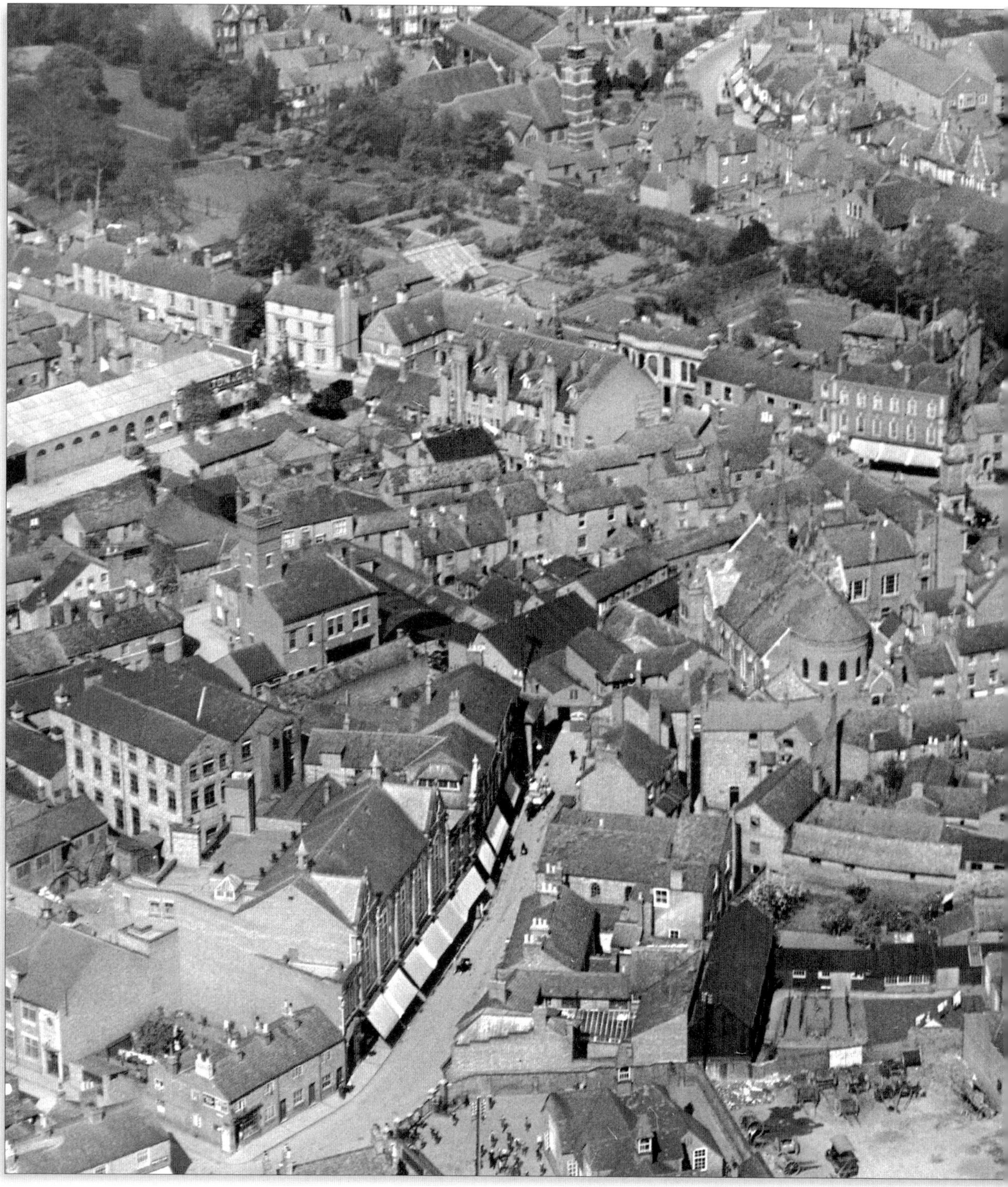

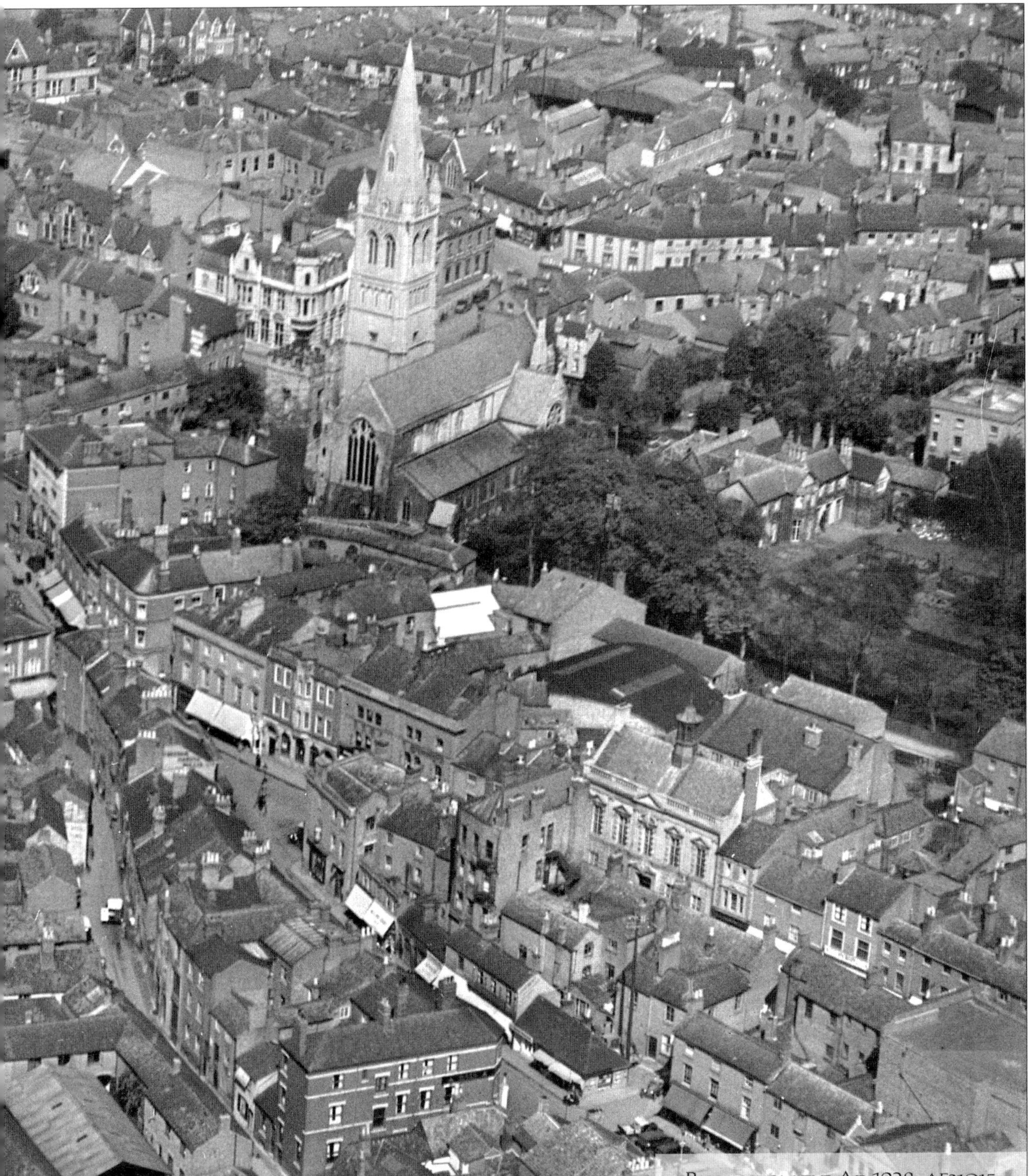

Rugby from the Air 1928 AF21015

INTRODUCTION

RUGBY lies on high table land in the Avon Valley, one of the huge river valleys formed at the end of the Ice Age when millions of gallons of water were released by melting glaciers. The soil — glacial drift over lias clays and limestones — is more suited to grass than grain, but in a land otherwise covered by dense forests, the valley's fertility and accessibility would have encouraged early settlement.

There is little archaeological evidence of pre-Bronze Age occupation in Rugby, although bones and Stone Age tools have been found nearby. Tumuli, or burial mounds, however, provide evidence of Bronze Age settlement, as does a bronze dagger found near Lawford Road.

When the Celts occupied Britain during the Iron Age, these tumuli were often incorporated into their fortifications, being used as platforms for beacon fires. Rugby may have been a small hill-fort of the Dobunni tribe overlooking a similar hill-fort occupied by the Coritani at Brownsover, the River Avon forming a boundary between the two, but more recent archaeology suggests that Rugby may have formed part of a network of villages stretching across the upper Avon Valley.

The name Rugby may well derive from the Celtic words 'droche', meaning 'rough' or 'wild', and 'brig', indicating a hilltop. Another ancient form, Rocheberie,

RUGBY SCHOOL, THE CLOSE 1922 72140

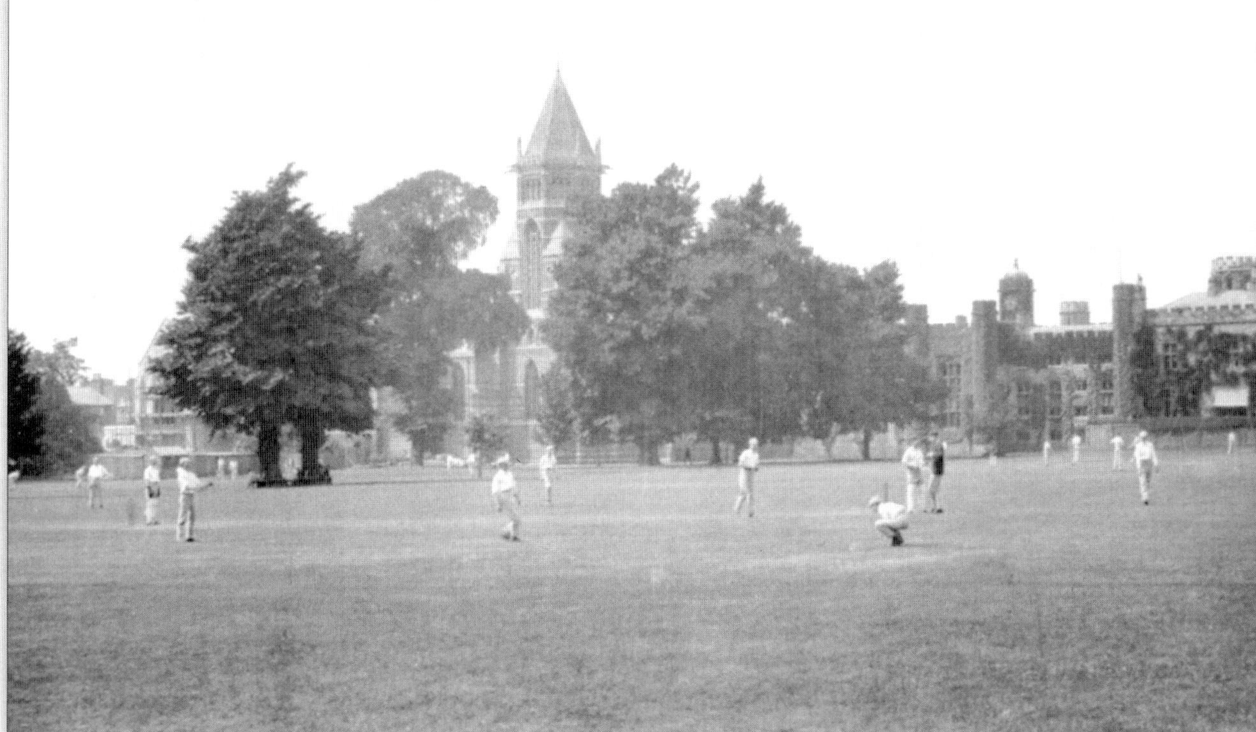

De.T.ten un pbr.i.virg træ.in ipſa uilla.Ibi.ē.i.car cū.i.
uitto.7 ibi.ii.ac pti.Valuit.v,ſol.Modo.x.ſol.
De.T.ten Eddulf in *ROCHEBERIE*.ii.hid 7 dim.Tra.ē.vi.car.
In dnio.ē.i.car.7 ii.ſerui.7 xi.uitti 7 v.bord cū.v.car.
Ibi molin de.xiii.ſol.7 iiii.denar.7 xvi.ac pti.Valuit.l.ſol.
Modo.xl.ſolid.
De.T.ten Vlf in *CALVESTONE*.i.hid.Tra.ē.i.car.Ipſa.ē
in dnio.7 iiii.uitt 7 i.bord 7 i.ſeru.Valuit.x.ſol.Modo.xii.ſol.

This extract from the Farley Text (1783) records, in much-abbreviated Latin, the entry for Rochberie in the Domesday Book of 1086.

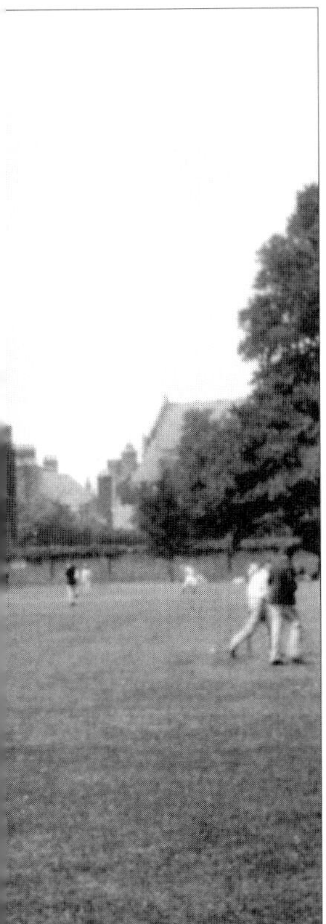

has been interpreted as 'important place' ('roche') and 'stone' ('berie'), and this was the name by which the area was known in mediaeval times, changing to Rokeby during the reign of Edward I.

There have been no significant Roman finds in Rugby, although at Tripontium, 4 miles to the east, a thriving Roman community grew up on either side of Watling Street (the A5). The Romans also improved an old trackway (the Fosse Way) 5 miles west of Rugby. This greater accessibility meant that by the time the Saxons arrived in the area during the 4th century, Rugby was probably already a well-established trading centre. Saxon villages such as Clifton, Bilton, Newbold and Long Lawford soon sprang up around the older town.

No Saxon chronicle makes any reference to Rocheberie, but after the Norman Conquest (1066), Rugby was still held by a Saxon nobleman, Turchil, whose family retained the manor throughout the 11th and 12th centuries.

The enclosures of the 15th and 16th centuries brought Rugby greater prominence, but in 1663 there were still only 160 houses in the town, rising to 183 by 1730, when the population stood at about 900. By 1831, however, the town's population had risen to 2,300, a dramatic increase attributable to the growing influence of the old Grammar School, known today as Rugby School.

Everything changed in 1838 when the London-Birmingham railway opened. Rugby's geographical position ('in the middle, where it matters') and excellent railway network brought rapid industrial growth, and by 1911 the population had soared to 21,758.

Market town, industrial centre and home of Rugby School: by the beginning of the 20th century Rugby was well and truly on the map.

RUGBY SCHOOL

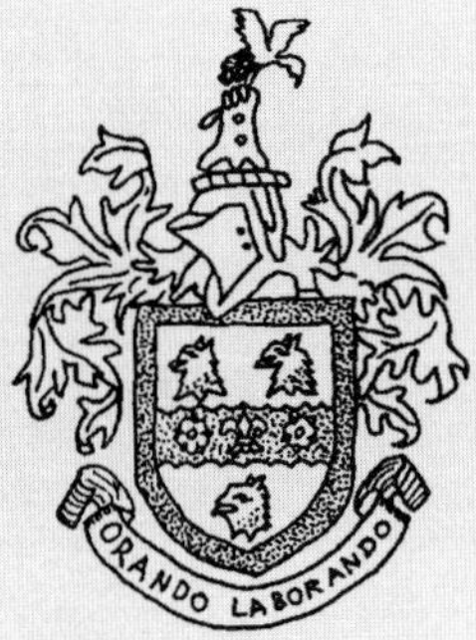

RUGBY SCHOOL COAT OF ARMS

The arms granted to Rugby School in 1932 are those of Lawrence Sheriff, but for the golden border and the roses in the lion's paw. The fleur-de-lis and the roses represent his service to the Royal House of Tudor; the griffins, 'fabled guardians of the treasures of the East', and the branch of dates in the lion's paw indicate the commodities in which he dealt. The motto translates as 'by prayer and work'.

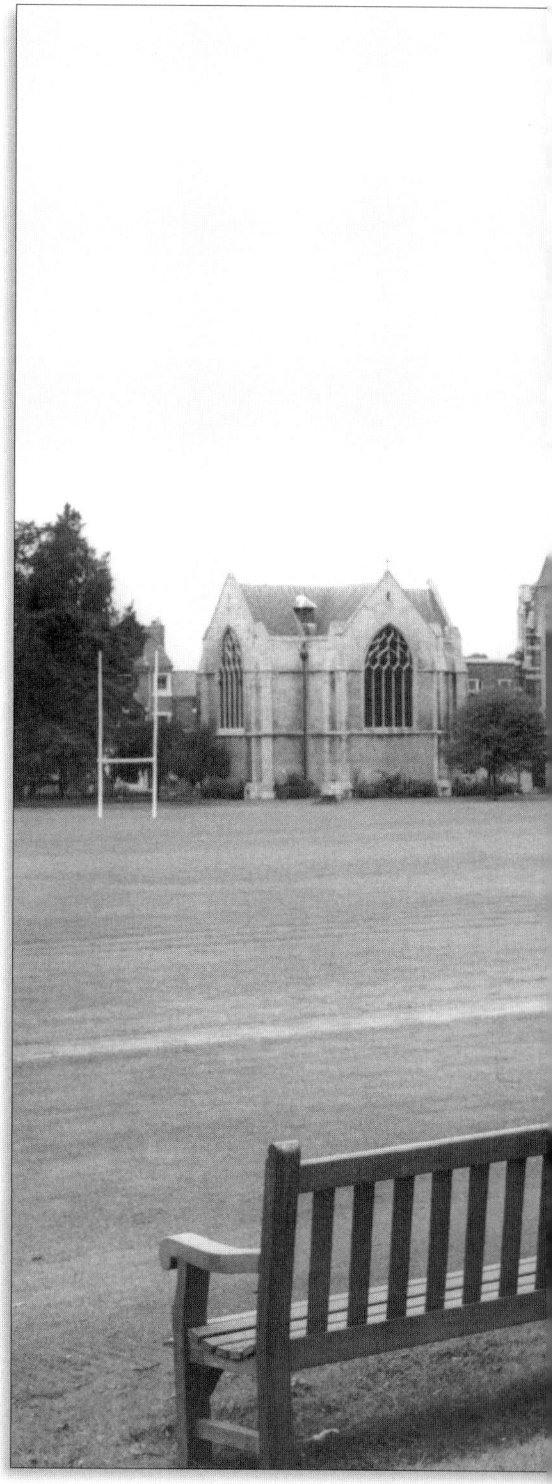

RUGBY SCHOOL, THE CLOSE c1965 R69079

This view shows Rugby School's First XV Rugby pitch, known as Old Big Side. The Memorial Chapel (left) was built in 1923. The main chapel, originally designed by Hakewell but completed by Butterfield, was built between 1818-1821. The oldest existing school buildings are School House (centre right) and the Headmaster's House (far right), built in 1815 in Elizabethan style as a tribute to Lawrence Sheriff. It was here on the Close, during a game of football in 1823, that William Webb Ellis picked up the ball and ran with it towards the tryline, thereby creating the new game of rugby. Here, too, a famous school rebellion took place, leading to a siege on the 'Island', out of camera shot on the far left of the Close. The Close is entered from Barby Road by gates commemorating the School's 4th centenary and dedicated by Queen Elizabeth II in 1967. To their left lies a mound created by a Second World War air raid shelter.

Rugby School

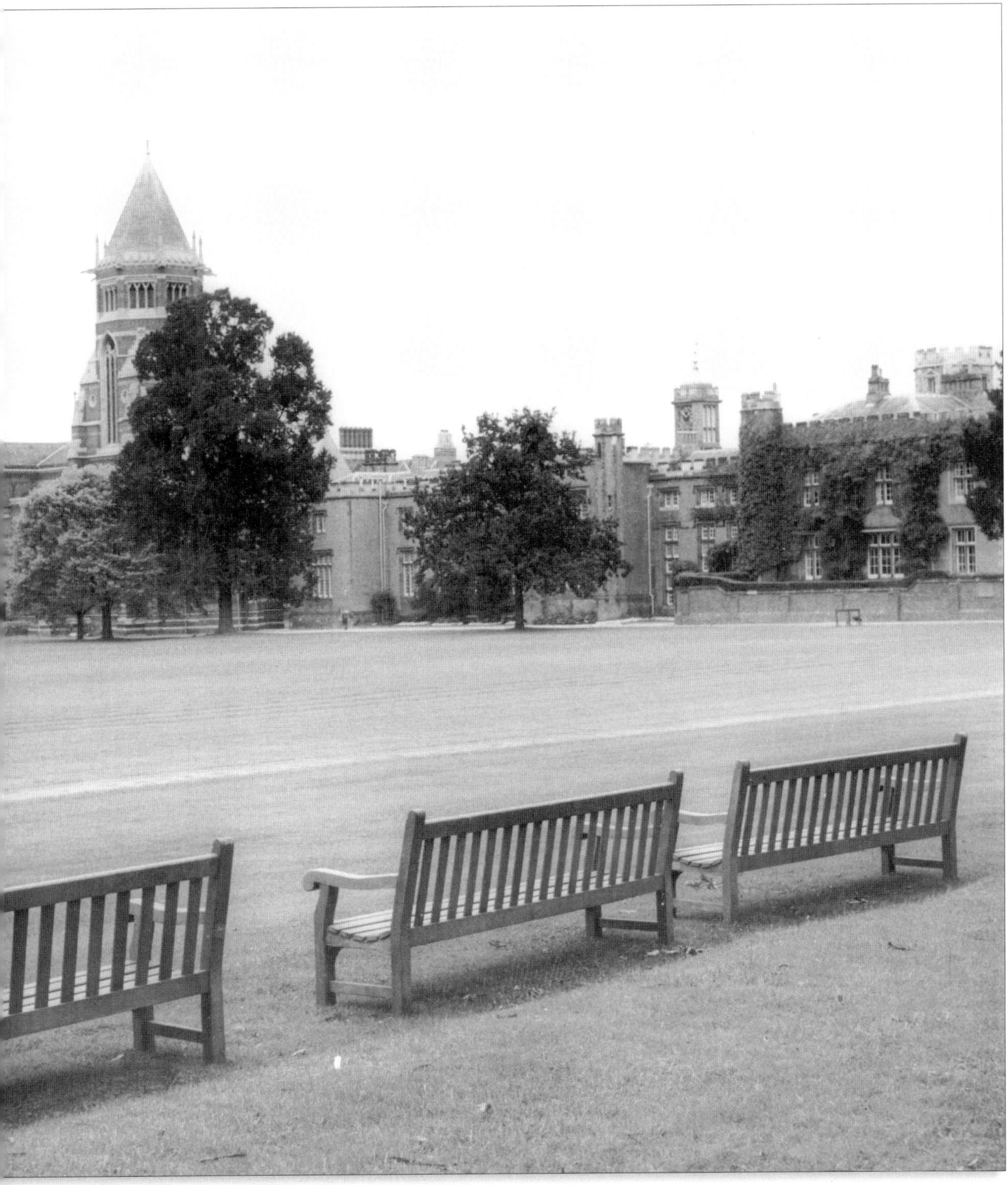

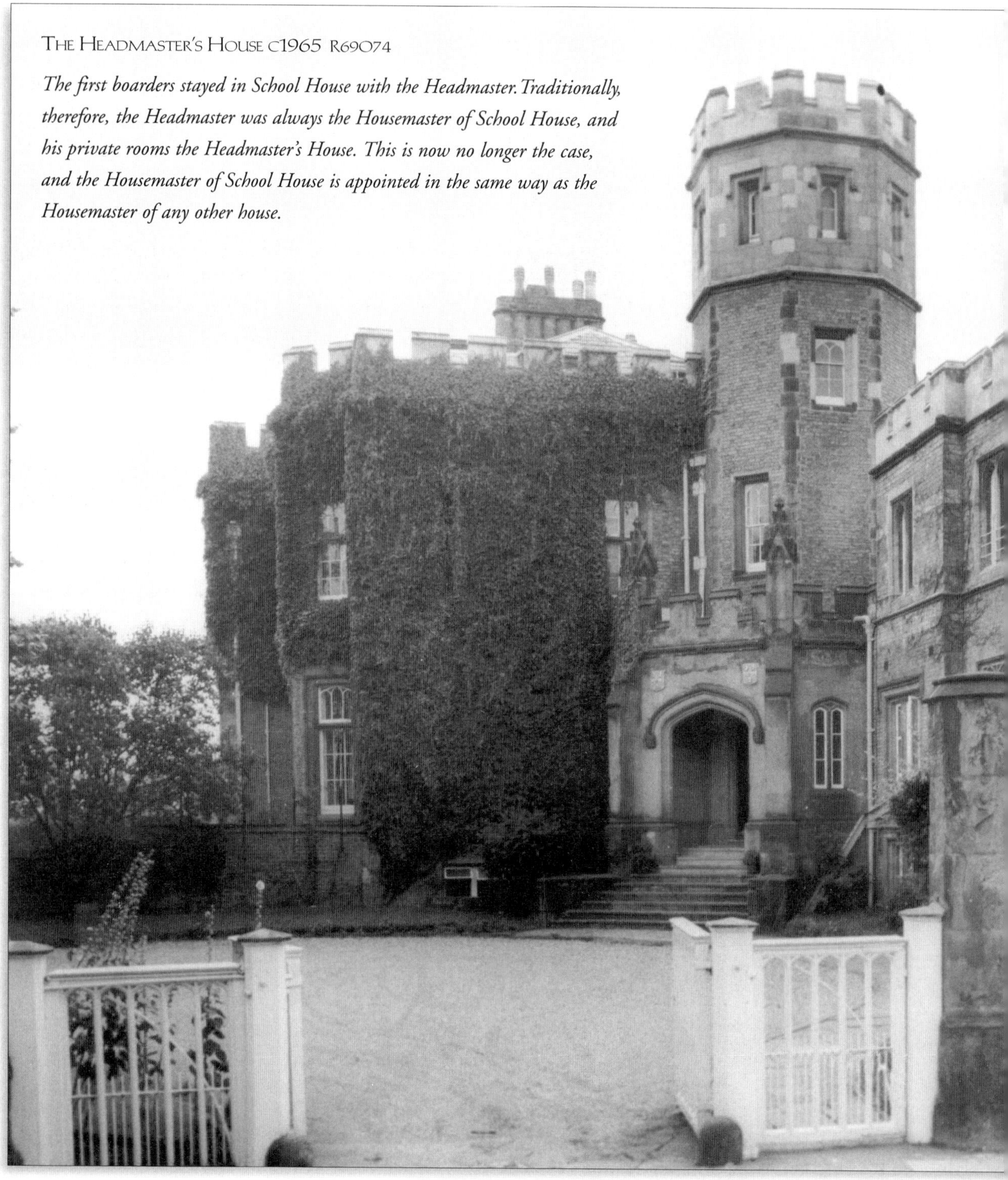

The Headmaster's House c1965 R69074

The first boarders stayed in School House with the Headmaster. Traditionally, therefore, the Headmaster was always the Housemaster of School House, and his private rooms the Headmaster's House. This is now no longer the case, and the Housemaster of School House is appointed in the same way as the Housemaster of any other house.

Rugby School

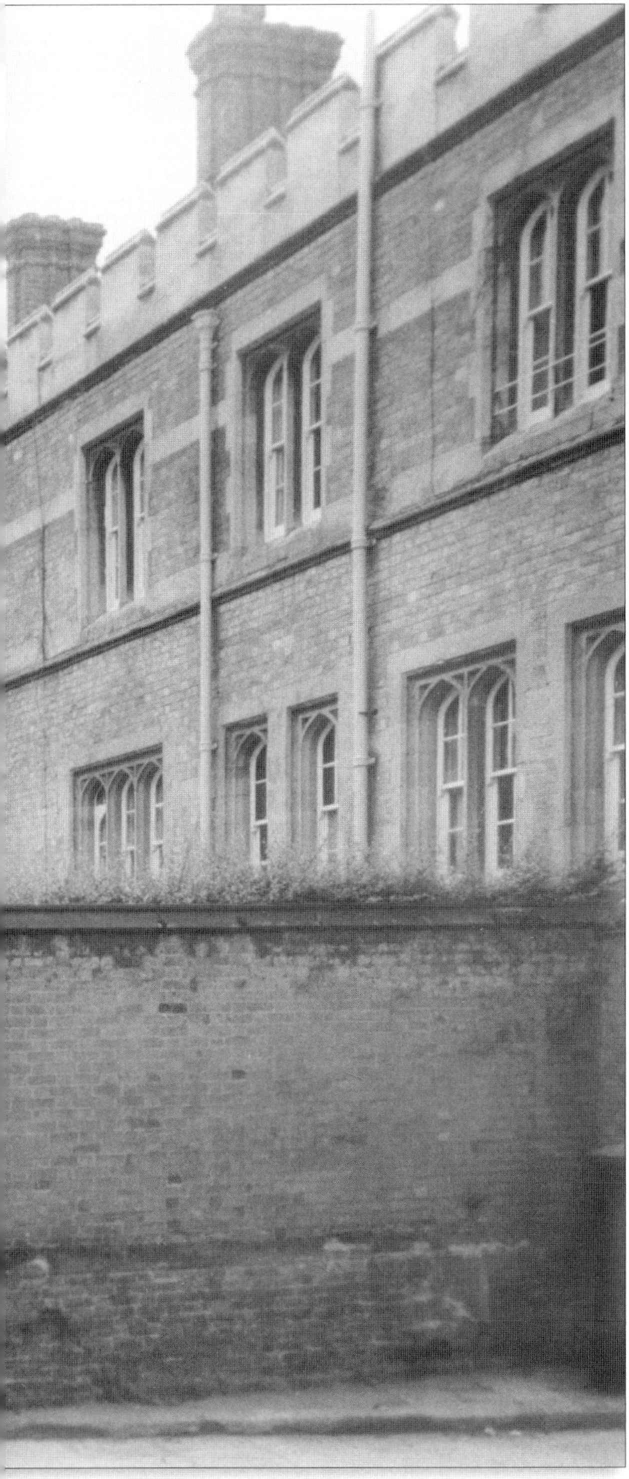

LAWRENCE SHERIFF, founder of Rugby School, was born in Rugby in about 1515. Apprenticed to a London grocer, he spent the rest of his life in London, supplying the household of Princess Elizabeth (later Queen) with 'spices and necessaries'. Elizabeth seems to have held him in some affection: in 1562 she gave him 'one gilt salt with a cover (weighing 7 oz)' in return for his gift of 'a sugar loaf, a box of ginger, a box of nutmegs and a pound of cinnamon'. In 1559, she rewarded him with a grant of arms.

In 1567, Lawrence Sheriff made a will leaving land and property for the foundation of four Rugby almshouses and a free Grammar School for boys from Rugby and Brownsover. In a later codicil he exchanged a cash sum for 8 acres of Lamb's Conduit Fields in Middlesex, a property that has contributed enormously to the School's finances. Lawrence Sheriff died two weeks after completing his will, but despite his wish to be buried at St Andrew's, he was buried at Greyfriars Church in London.

The original school, opposite the parish church, was completed in 1574. It was two-storeyed at the front, with living accommodation for a master and four almsmen, but the schoolroom at the rear was just one long, high room, built of wood, lath and plaster. The boys played on a small piece of land near the church and, unofficially, in the churchyard as well.

Edward Rolston was the first master, with a salary of £12 per year; but later decades saw much turmoil in the school administration until a new body of Trustees was set up in 1653. High academic standards had been maintained, however, and non-foundationers (fee-paying boarders) were now being admitted. By 1675, nearly half of the 26 boys at the school were non-foundationers, requiring a second storey to be built over the school. The School's reputation for excellence grew, and during the Mastership of Henry Holyoake (1687-1731) the sons of noblemen and baronets began to appear on the register.

Rugby School

By 1740 the original premises were very dilapidated; the Manor House at the south end of High Street was purchased for £1,000 to provide a new Master's House. A new school, very similar in design to the old school, was built on the site of the present School House Hall (School House is shown in R69026, right).

In 1777 an Act of Parliament allowed for the founding of Exhibitions and the appointment of assistant masters, and thus in 1778 Dr Thomas James became the first Headmaster. A firm disciplinarian and a fine classical scholar, Dr James introduced a tutorial system, along with praeposters or monitors, served by fags, and Dames' houses in the town, where boys could board. By 1790 the school roll had soared to 240.

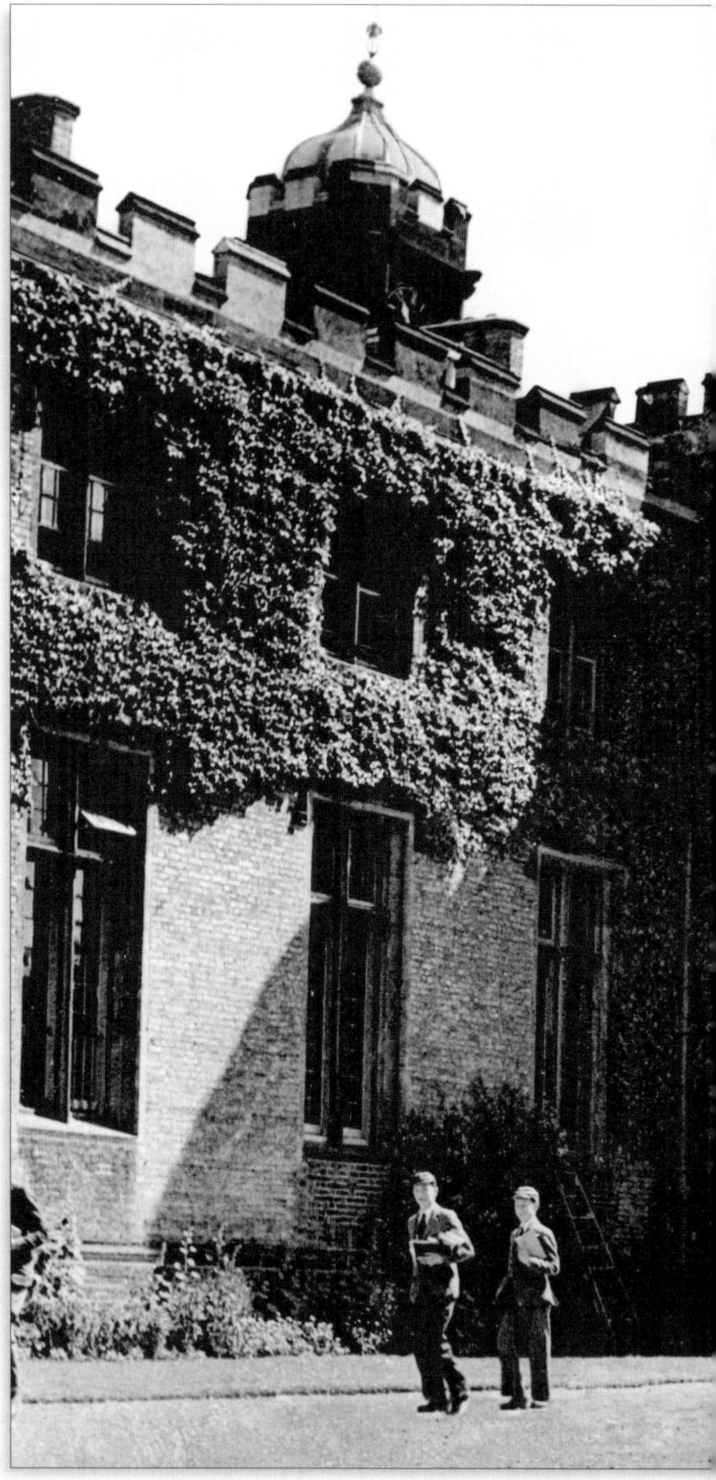

School House c1955 R69026

School House, built between 1809-1813 on the site of the 1740 new school, was the first school boarding house. Many boys lodged at Dames' houses throughout the town, but this had certain disadvantages, as this report notes:

'During the great November horse fair, when the streets were thronged with horses, and there were no barriers to keep them off the footpaths, the boarding-houses being for the most part scattered over the town, such inmates of them as were in the First and Second Forms, who although they might be giants in Literature — a fact greatly to be doubted — being not so in size, were judiciously kept out of School and confined to their respective boarding-houses'.

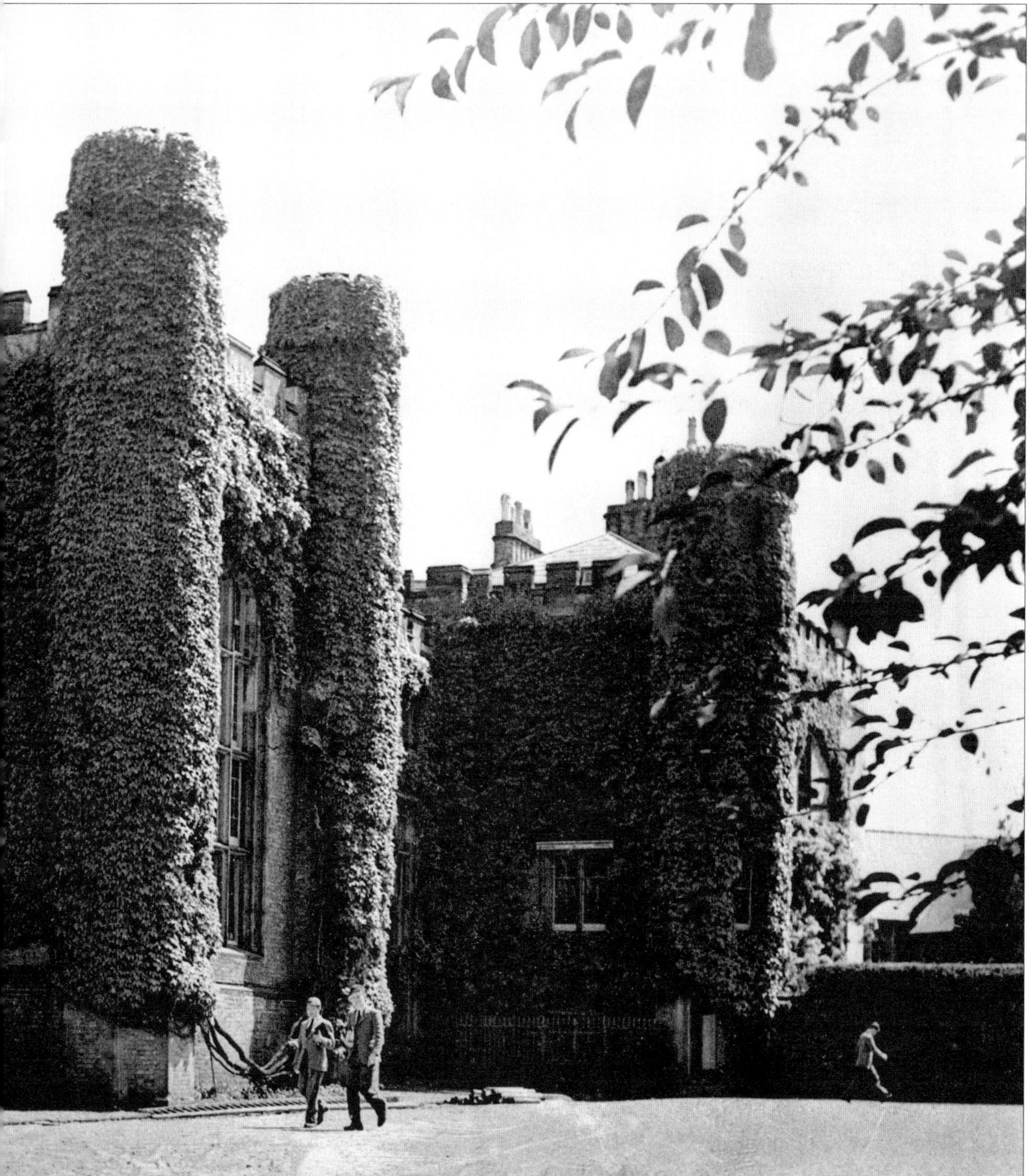

Rugby School

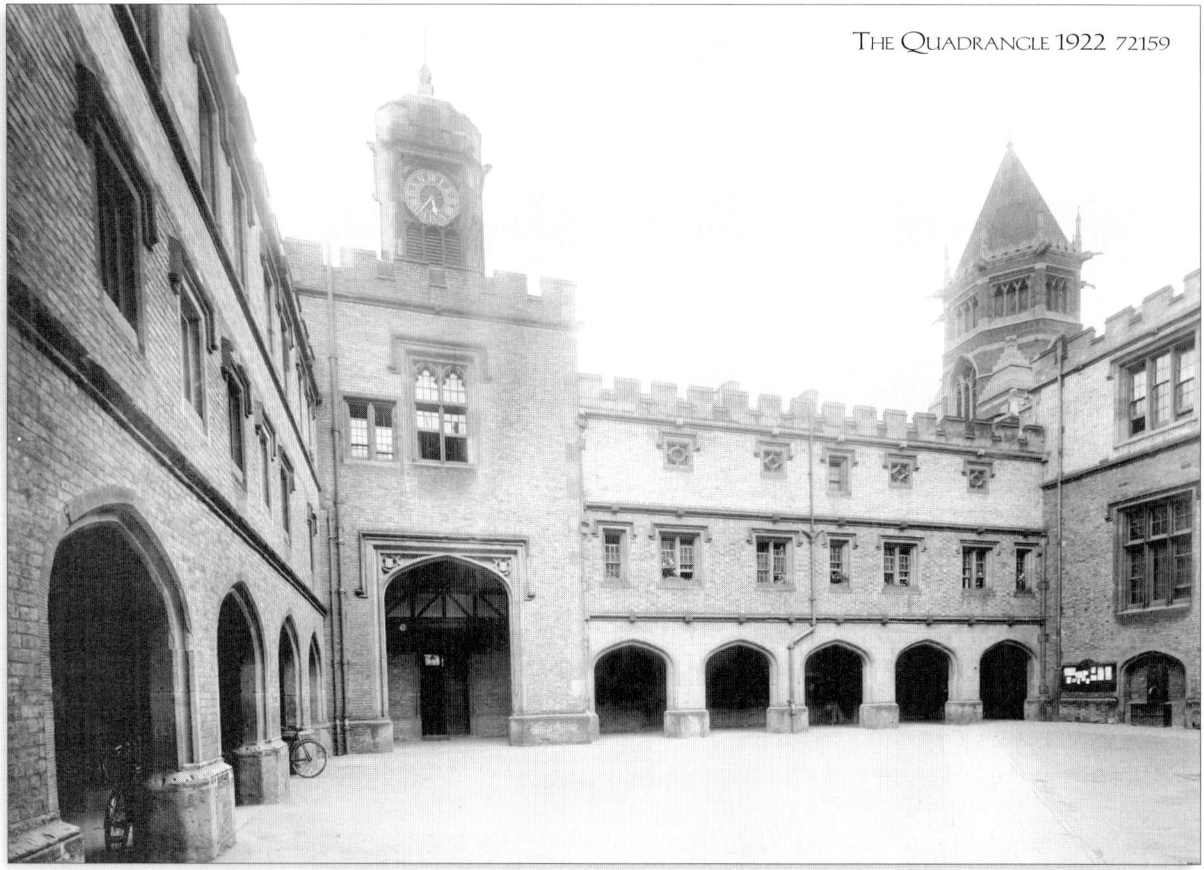

The Quadrangle 1922 72159

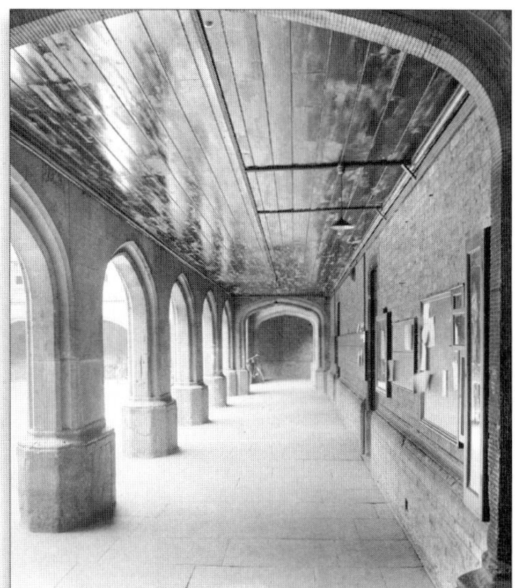

Right: The Cloisters 1922 72160

To the west of Old Quad (above, 72159) lies Old Big School, surmounted by School House dormitories. In the shallow recess stands a pump which was used by the boys to collect their washing water until washrooms and indoor toilets were installed in 1922. The lozenge-shaped washroom windows can be seen (centre, 72159) on the south side of Old Quad. Cloisters with studies above run to the south and east of Old Quad, with a tall arch forming the entrance to the School House dining hall at the south-eastern corner. Through the Cloisters to the south-west lies the Birching Tower, used until corporal punishment ceased in the 1960s. The Clock Tower was visible from High Street until the Headmaster's School was built over the gateway in 1830. Some 100-150 books donated by Henry Holyoake disappeared mysteriously from the Tower between 1858 and 1870.

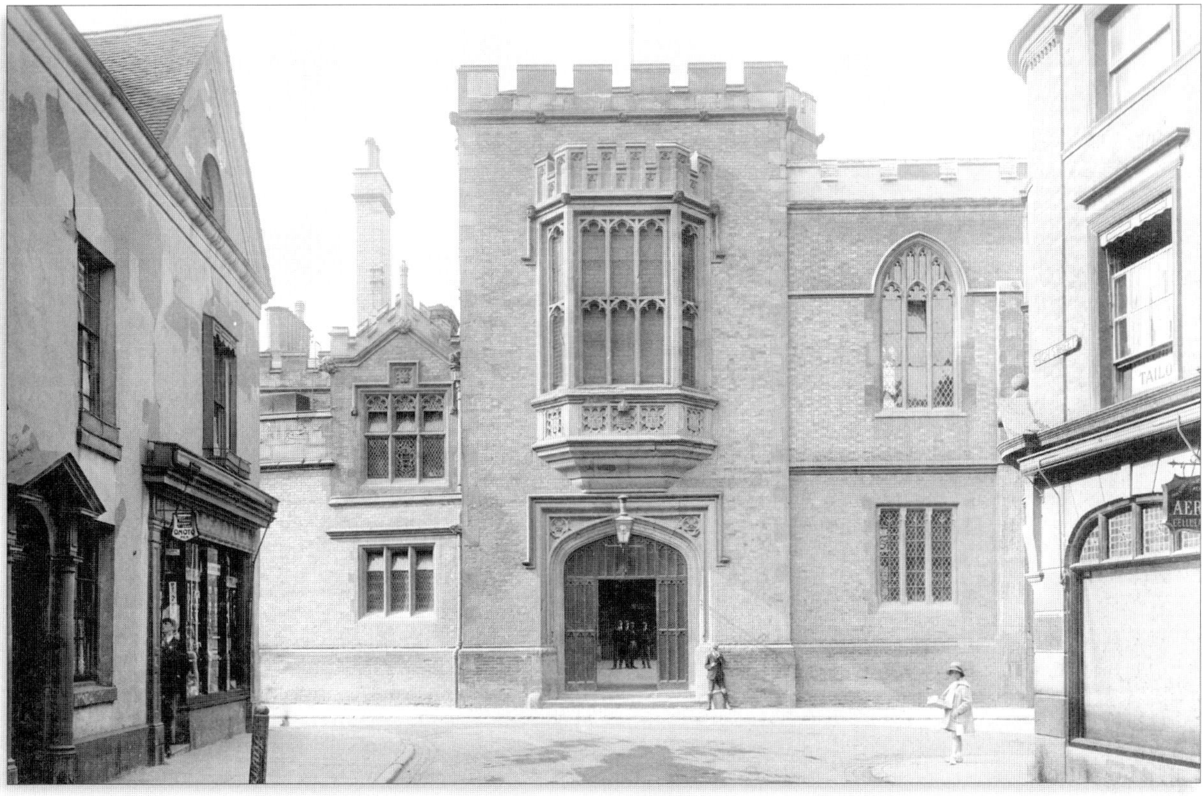

THE GATEWAY 1922 72153

Dr J Percival, (Headmaster 1887-1895) donated the window above the gateway to Old Quad which looks down onto the High Street. Its stained glass bears the names and portraits of successive Headmasters until 1894. To its right lies the Arnold Library, built as a memorial to Dr Arnold in 1842.

Dr James was not one to spare the rod, but his successor, Dr Henry Ingles, was known as 'The Black Tiger' for the severity of his rule. His headmastership is best remembered for the Great Rebellion of 1797. Dr Ingles was walking in the town when he heard pistol shots. A boy from the school, Astley, claimed that Mr Rowell, a grocer, had supplied him with gunpowder for a cork gun. Rowell denied this, and Astley was flogged as a liar. Astley, with his friends, retaliated by smashing Rowell's windows. Dr Ingles ordered that the Fifth and Sixth Forms pay for the damage. This provoked a riot in which Dr Ingles's door was blown off, windows were broken, and desks, benches and books were burned on the Close.

Dr Ingles summoned help from the town. A party of recruiting soldiers and townsfolk advanced on the rioters, who took refuge on the Island (a Bronze Age tumulus on the Close, surrounded at this time by a moat complete with drawbridge). The Riot Act was read and the boys were called upon to surrender, but this was merely a diversion enabling the soldiers to wade across the moat at the rear and take the whole party prisoner.

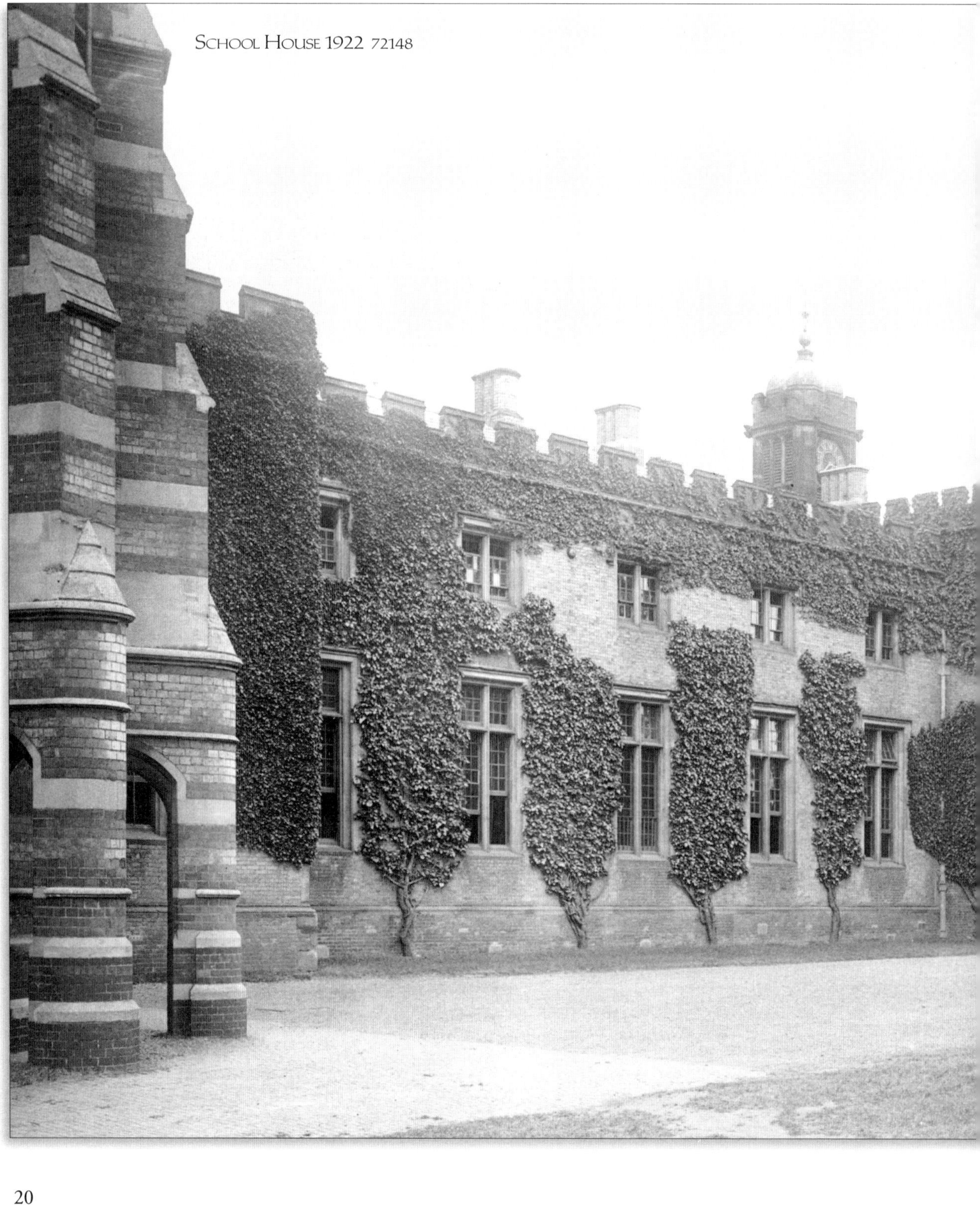

School House 1922 72148

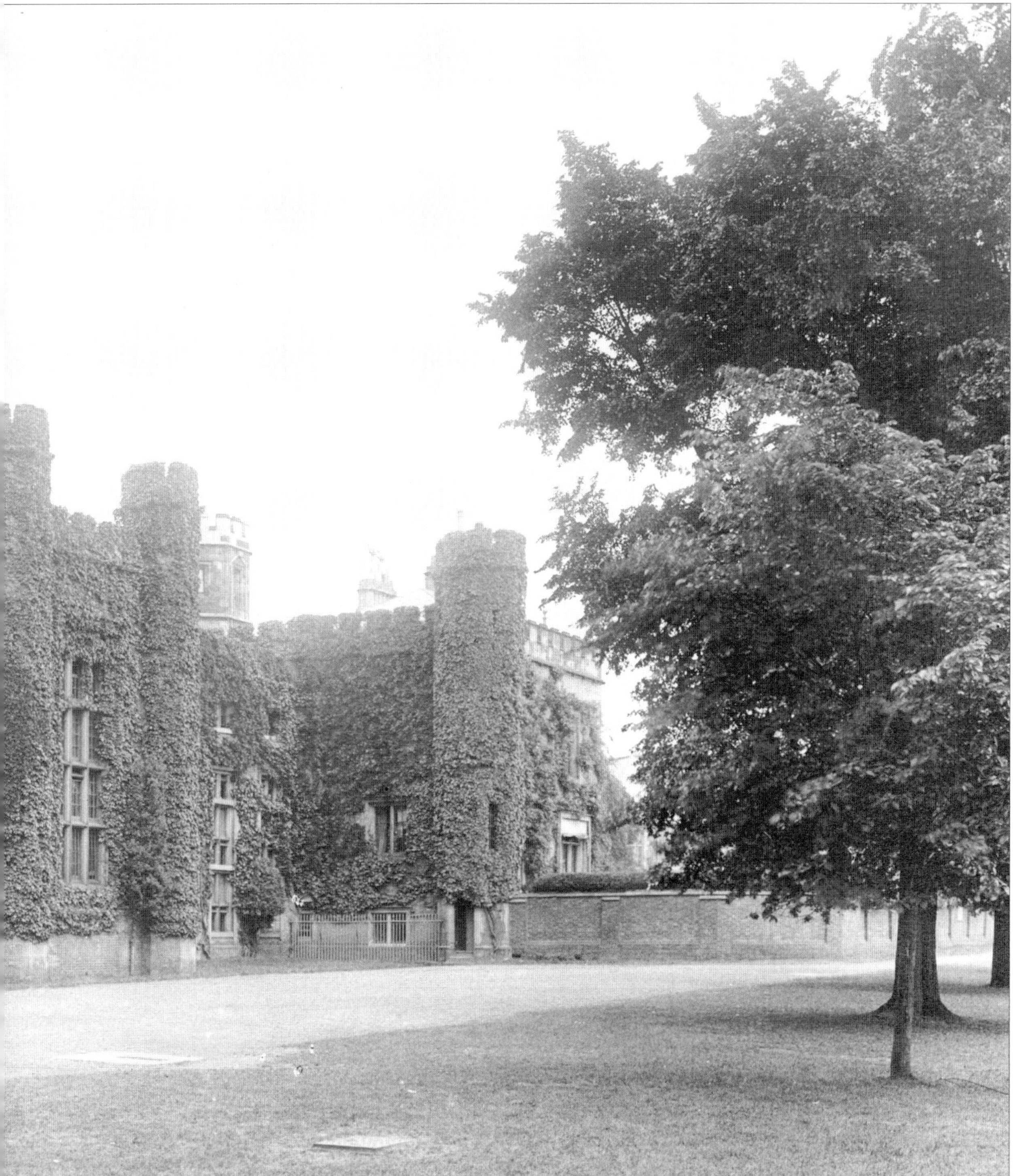

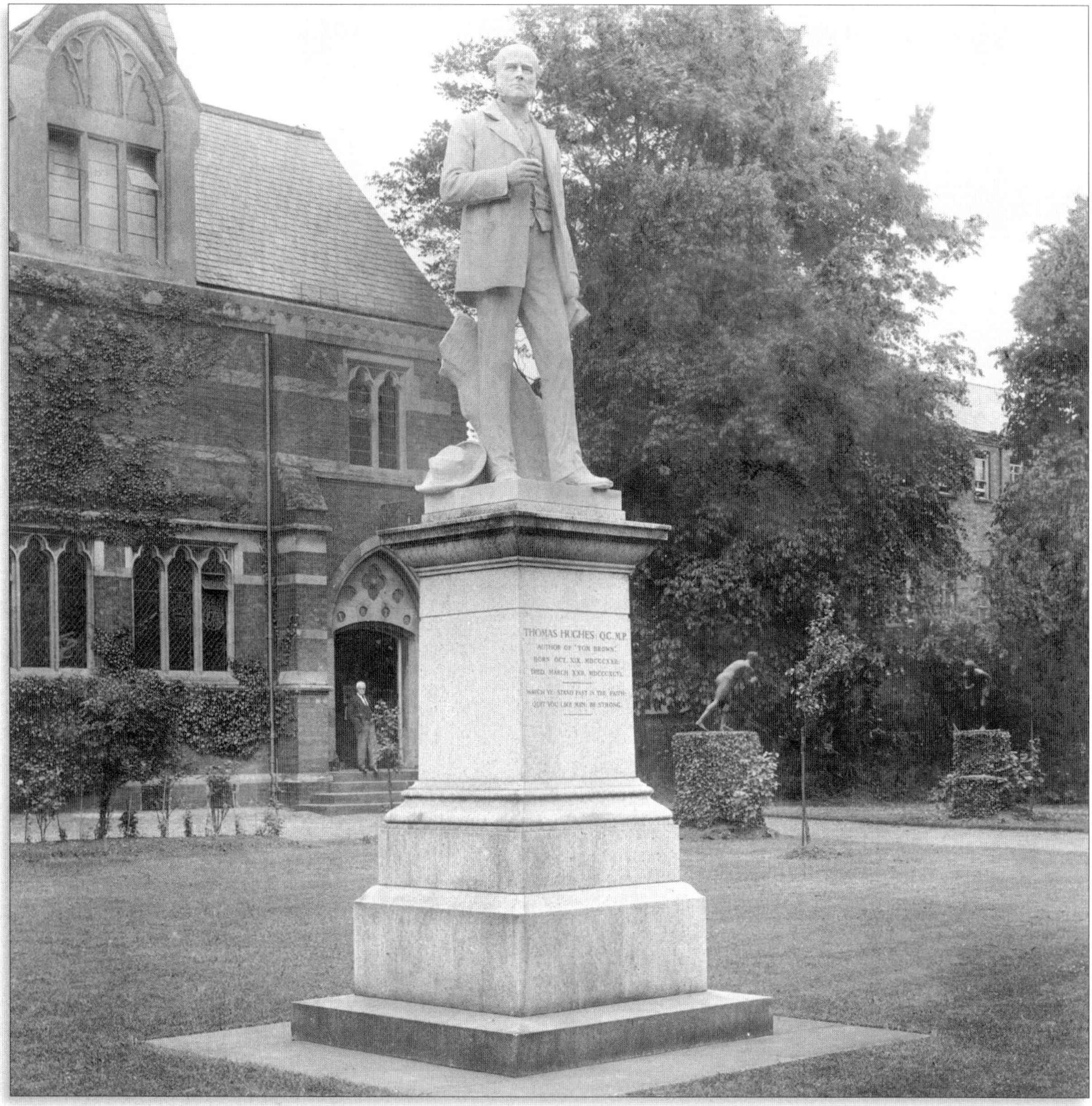

THOMAS HUGHES STATUE 1922 72152

This white marble monument by Thomas Brock stands outside the Temple Reading Room on Barby Road. Unveiled in 1899 by Edward Benson, Archbishop of Canterbury, the inscription reads:

*THOMAS HUGHES Q.C. M.P. | 'AUTHOR OF TOM BROWN' | BORN OCT XIX MDCCCXXII |
DIED MARCH XXII MDCCCXCVI | WATCH YE: STAND FAST IN THE FAITH: QUIT YE LIKE MEN: BE STRONG*

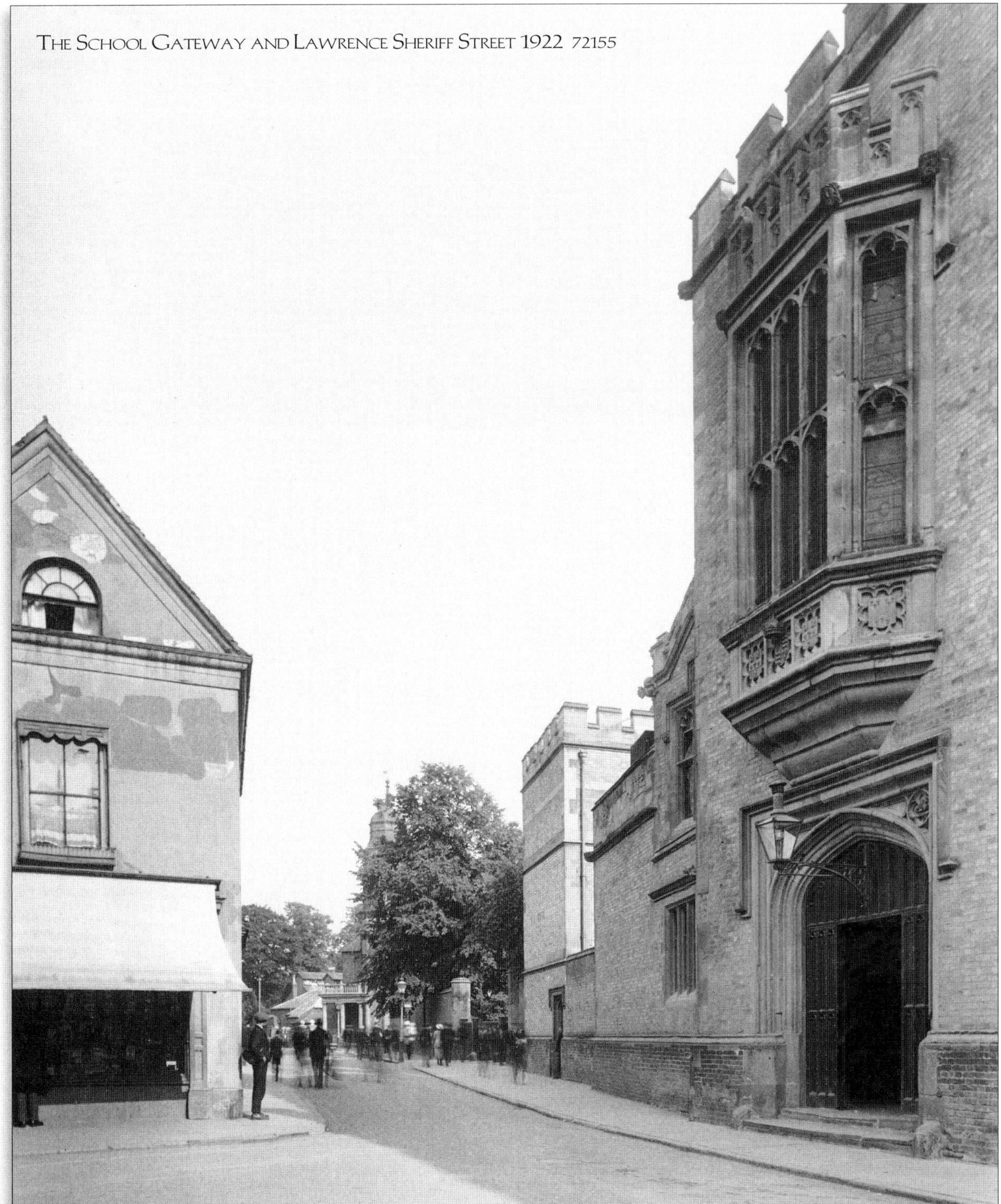

THE SCHOOL GATEWAY AND LAWRENCE SHERIFF STREET 1922 72155

Rugby School

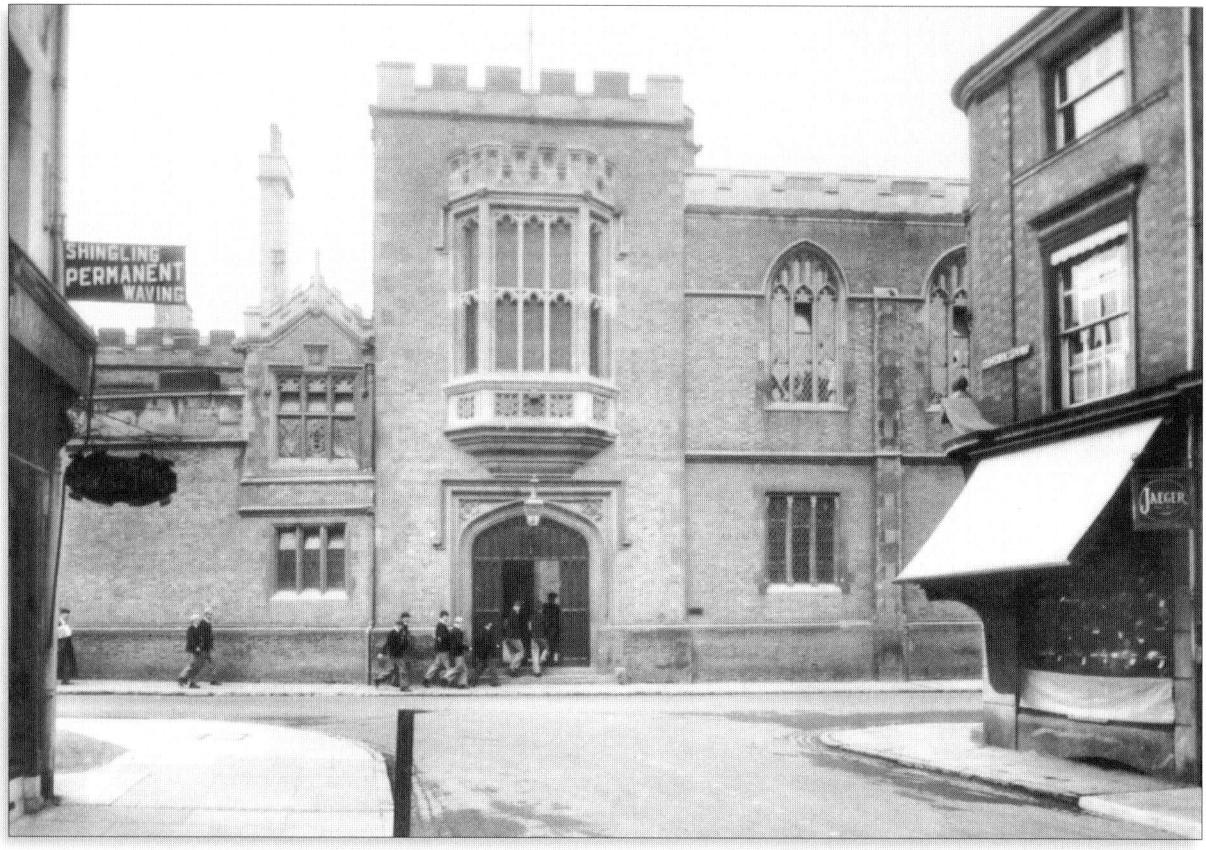

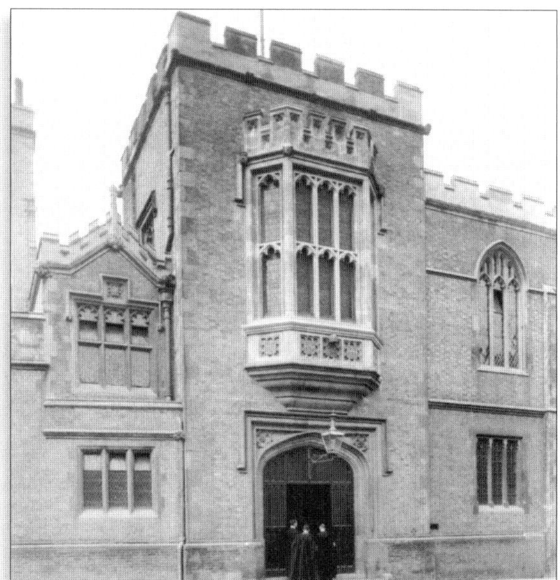

Above and Right: QUAD GATE 1932 85181, 85182

In Dr James's day there was no official uniform. The boys wore long, single-breasted coats, flowing waistcoats with slits at the hips, silk stockings and sealskin shoes with silver buckles. In the late 19th century, striped caps and Eton collars were the standard dress, the striped cap surviving well into the 20th century. The masters here wear academic gowns, a sight now seen only on formal occasions.

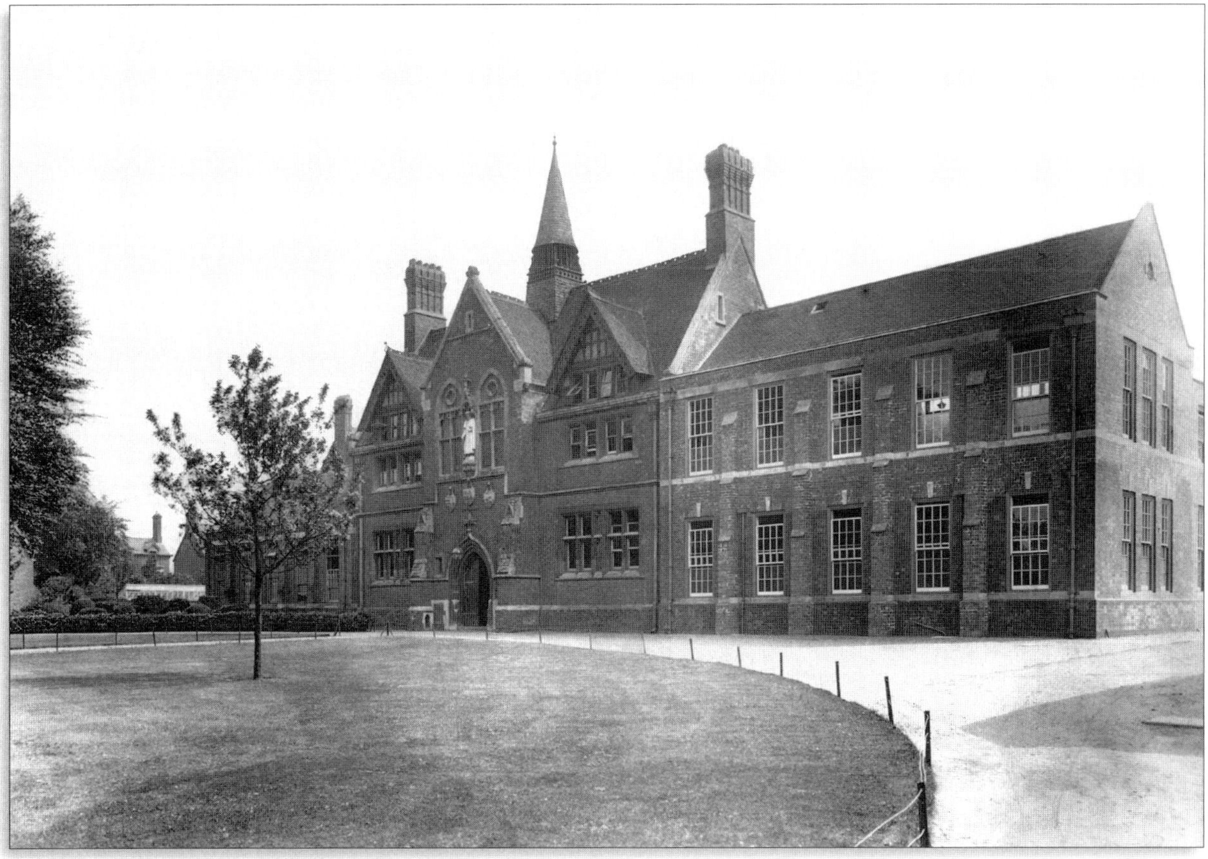

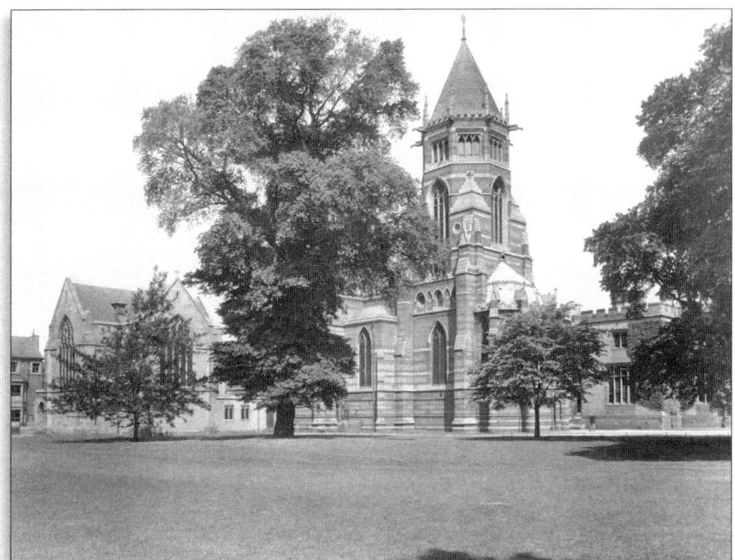

Above: Lawrence Sheriff School 1932 85190

Lawrence Sheriff School was opened in 1879 in response to Dr Temple's proposal in 1864 that a separate free school be established for local boys. It was built in mock Tudor style, and carries above the door a statue dressed in the livery of the Grocers' Company — a tribute to Lawrence Sheriff.

Left: The School Chapel 1932 85184

THE TEMPLE SPEECH ROOM 1922 72164

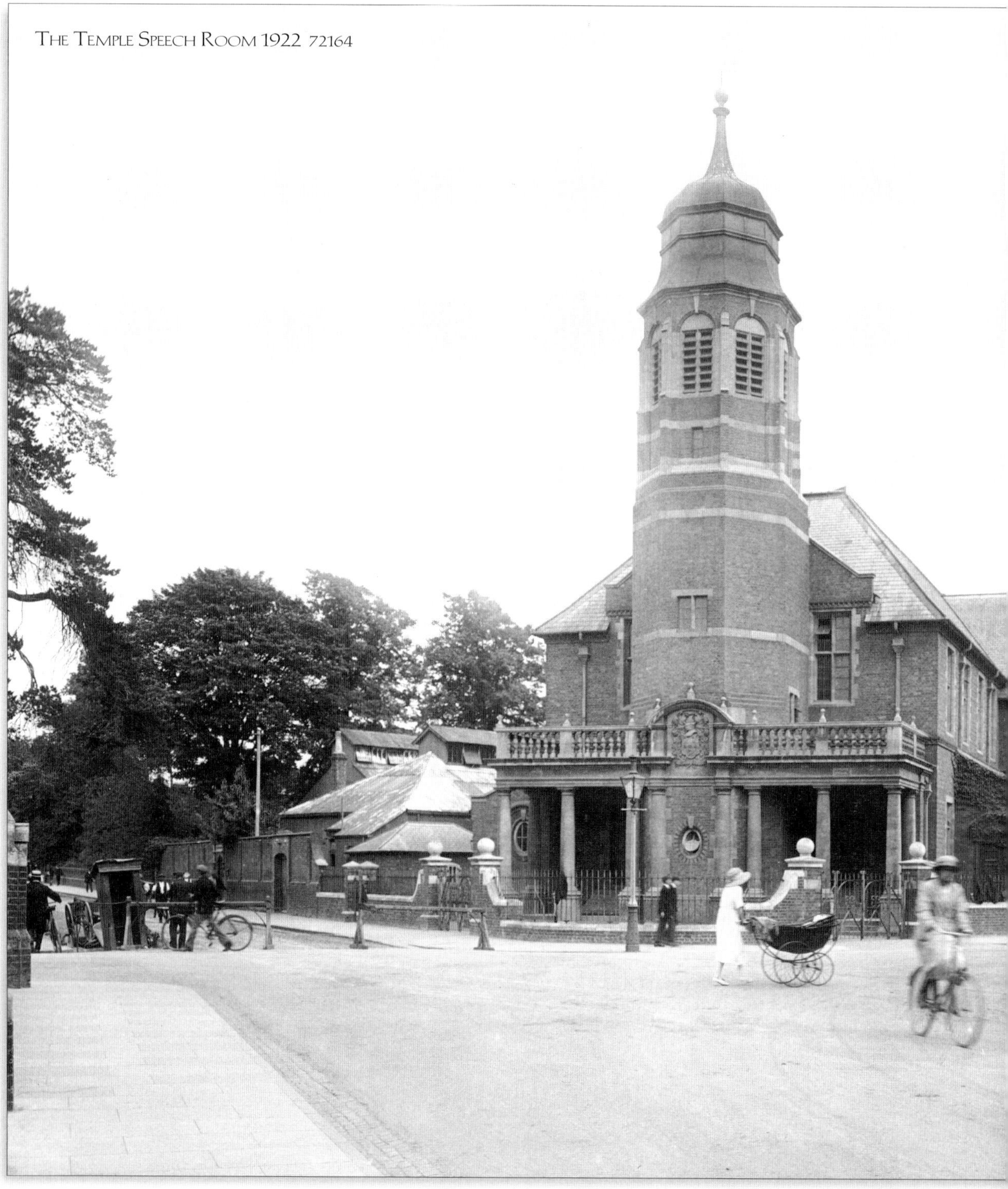

Rugby School

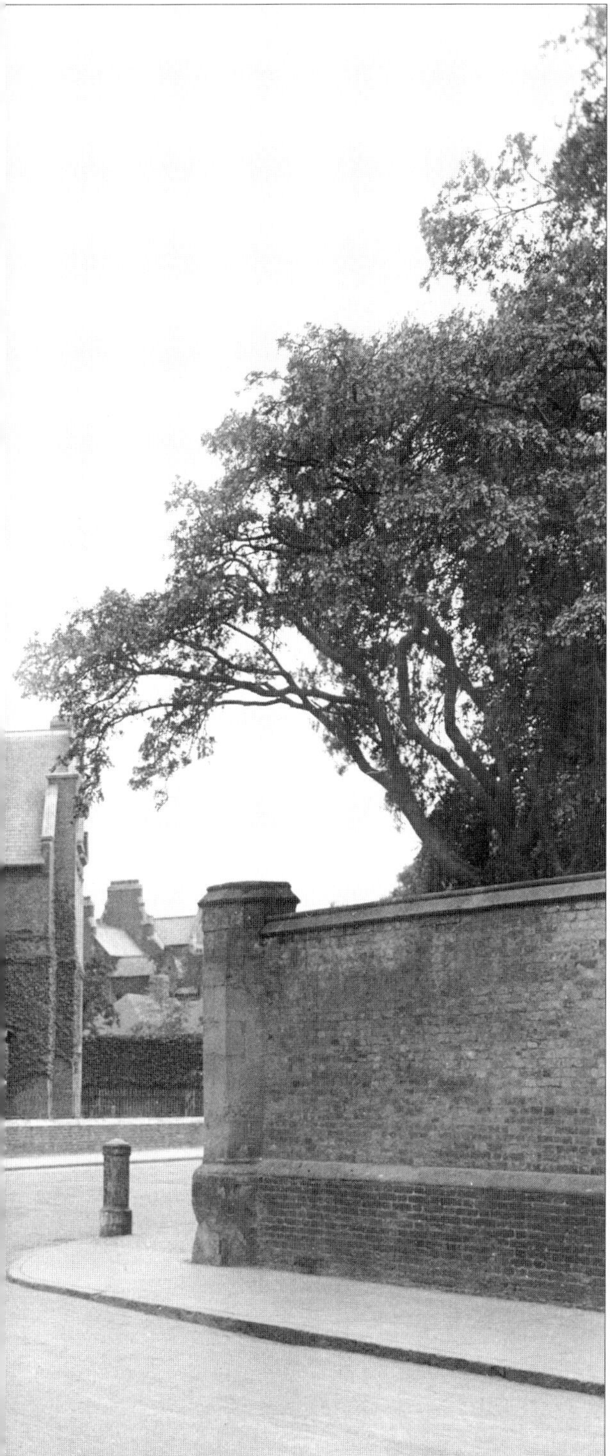

Dr John Wooll's headmastership (1806-1828) saw much rebuilding. The new buildings, designed by Henry Hakewell, were of white brick with stone dressings and battlements in a 15th-century style nicknamed 'Georgian Gothic'.

From 1821 onwards there was a dramatic rise in the number of wealthy families moving into Rugby so that their sons could be educated at the school. This led to the construction of many smart residential properties along Bilton Road, Hillmorton Road and Dunchurch Road, for example.

Thomas Arnold succeeded Dr Wooll in 1829, and his influence was to have a profound effect on both public and state school education. Thomas Hughes (see 72152, page 22) gives a graphic account of his headmastership in his famous novel 'Tom Brown's Schooldays'.

The Temple Reading Room (behind the statue) was designed by Butterfield and built by Parnell in 1879 at a cost of £9,000. Much of the cost was met by Dr Jex-Blake, the first Rugby School Headmaster to have been educated at the school. Its stained glass windows contain the names of those boys and masters who have become bishops. Now the School Library, the building once also housed the Art Museum. The second of the School's two 'Tin Tabernacles' (the Art School) once stood here among the trees where the History Department building now stands.

Dr Arnold's aim was to produce 'Christian gentlemen' by encouraging religious and moral principles, gentlemanly conduct and intellectual ability. Flogging remained the punishment for grave moral lapses, but Dr Arnold believed it better to train 'by influence and words', by explaining, praising and by raising self-esteem. Dr Arnold also made important changes to the curriculum, retaining the traditional classical studies but placing more emphasis on history, geography, English, maths and modern languages.

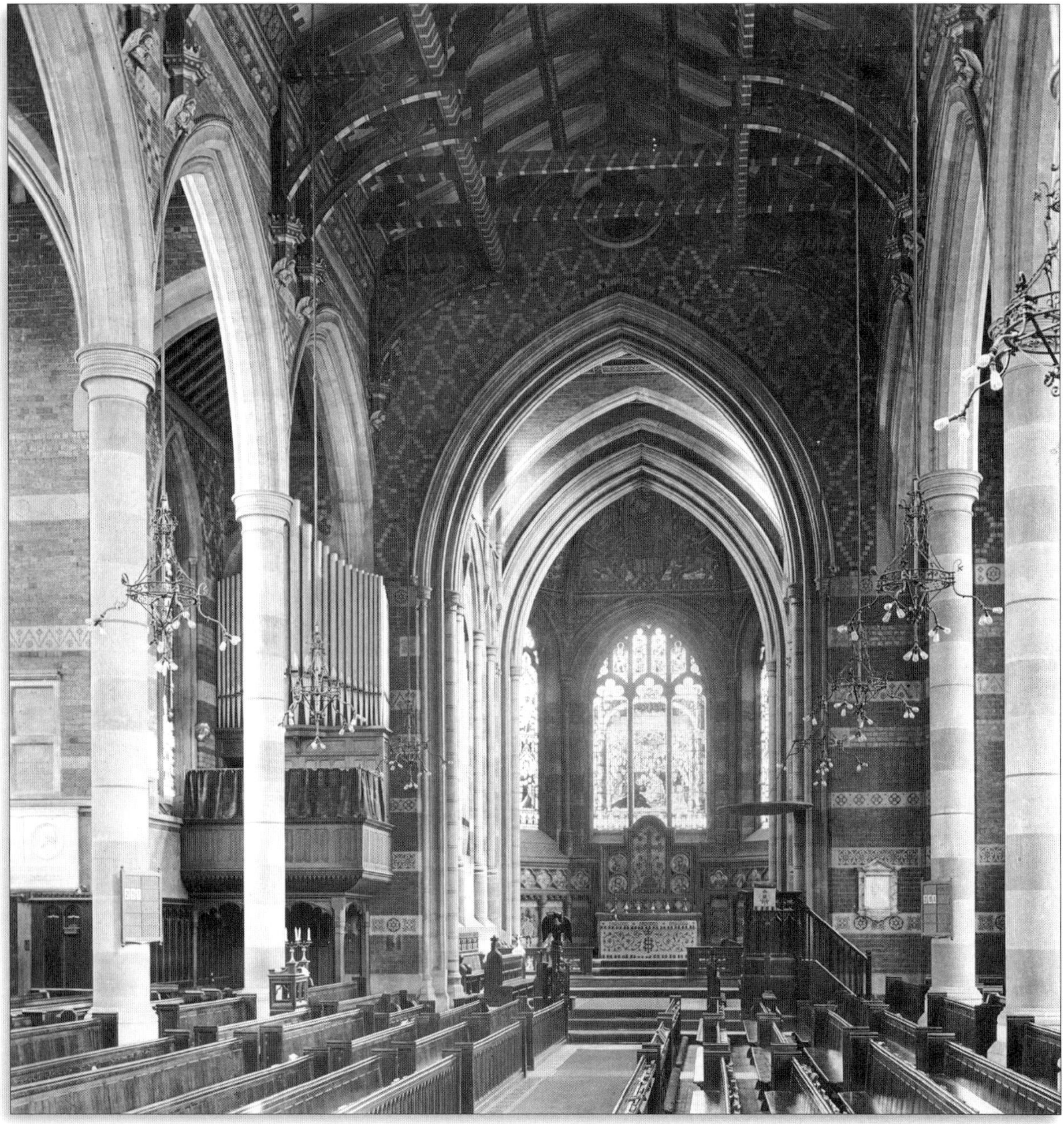

THE SCHOOL CHAPEL 1922 72161

The original flat plaster ceiling of the chapel was divided into squares by thin beams, each square being divided into four triangles with an elaborate wooden boss at each intersection. Dr Arnold hated this roof and would have been delighted that in 1852 it was replaced by this open timberwork ceiling.

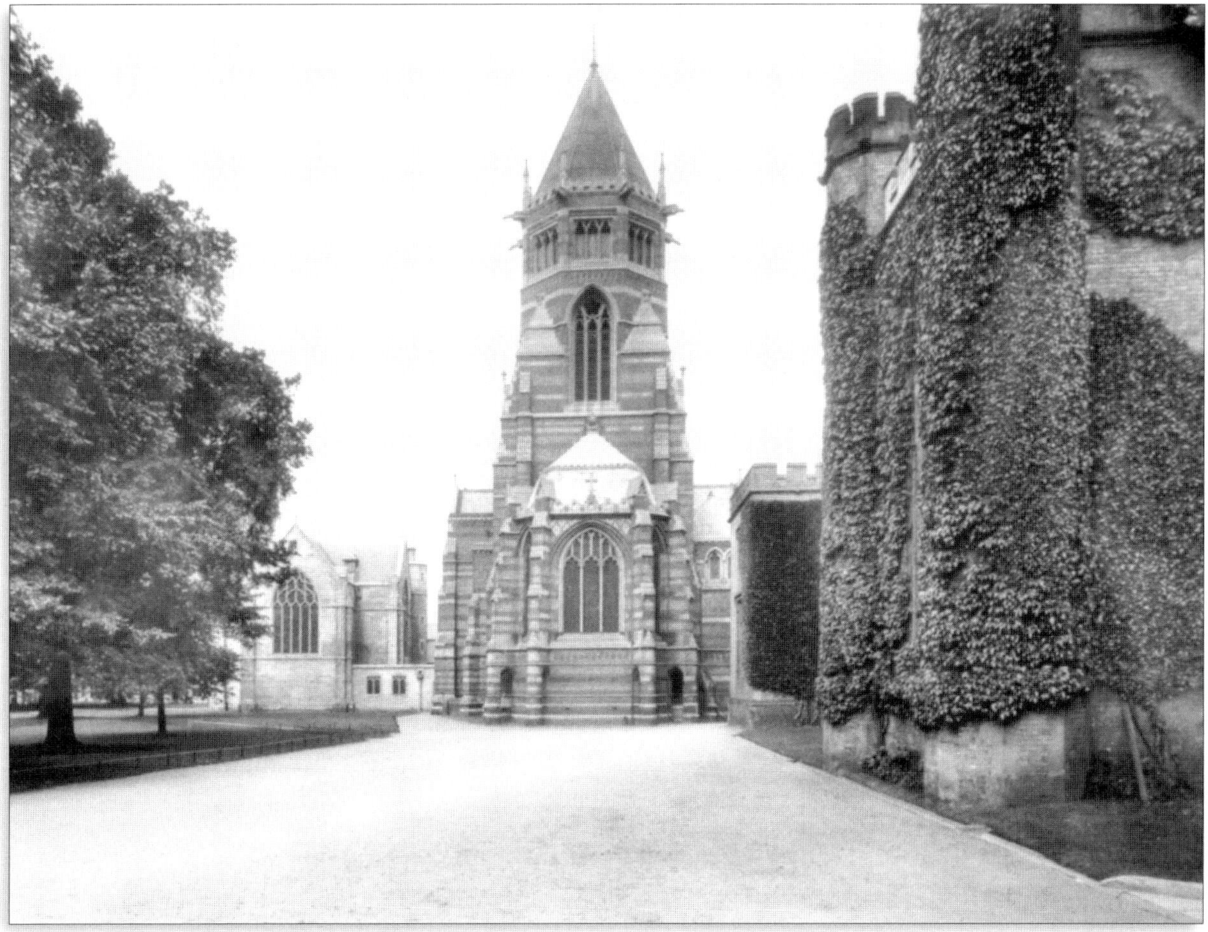

THE SCHOOL CHAPEL 1932 85183

RUGBY SCHOOL HALL OF FAME

Art, Music & Literature

Thomas Arnold
Matthew Arnold
Sir Arthur Bliss
Rupert Brooke
Arthur Hugh Clough
Charles Lutwidge Dodgson
TH Green (Philosopher)
Thomas Hughes
Walter Savage Landor
Wyndham Lewis
John Gillespie Magee
Sir Sydney Nicholson
Arthur Ransome
Salman Rushdie
RH Tawney

Science

Sir John Badenock
Professor Vero Wynne-Edwards

Stage, Screen & Sport

William Webb Ellis
Thomas Macready
Sir Anthony Quayle

Religion

Archbishop Tait
Archbishop Frederick Temple
Archbishop William Temple

Politics

Austen Chamberlain
Neville Chamberlain
RA Cross
Goschen
Edward Stanley
Lord Strauss
Lord Waddington

Dr Arnold ended the system of Dames' houses, replacing it with the House system and placing particular emphasis on pastoral care. He also closed the two lower forms, which were comprised of local boys between the ages of six and twelve. This controversial move went against the principle of Lawrence Sheriff's original foundation, but an 1868 Act of Parliament conferred on the governing body the right to limit the powers of the foundation. This led to the later establishment of the Subordinate School of Lawrence Sheriff (the Lower School — see 85190, page 25).

Rugby School

The headmastership of Frederick Temple (1858–1869), later Archbishop of Canterbury, saw much further building work carried out, including the New Quadrangle, the Gymnasium and the reconstruction of the School Chapel.

Since 1922, Lawrence Sheriff Street (72164, page 26-27) has seen a considerable increase in traffic. It is now a busy box junction, with a traffic island at the end of Barby Road. To the left stands one of the two metal-roofed buildings built in the second half of the 19th century and dubbed the 'Tin Tabernacles'. Originally the first science building, this was the Natural History Society Museum until it was replaced in 1925 by the Music Schools. The Temple Speech Room (72164, page 26-27) was built during the headmastership of Henry James (1895-1910). The interior was seriously damaged by fire in 1999, but has now been fully restored.

In 1814 the School Trustees were empowered by Act of Parliament to build a chapel, the cost not to exceed £800. Designed by Hakewell, it was built in 13th-century style with some Tudor features. Dr Wooll laid the first stone in 1818. In 1821 it was consecrated by Edward Legge, Bishop of Oxford and an Old Rugbeian, and dedicated to St Lawrence.

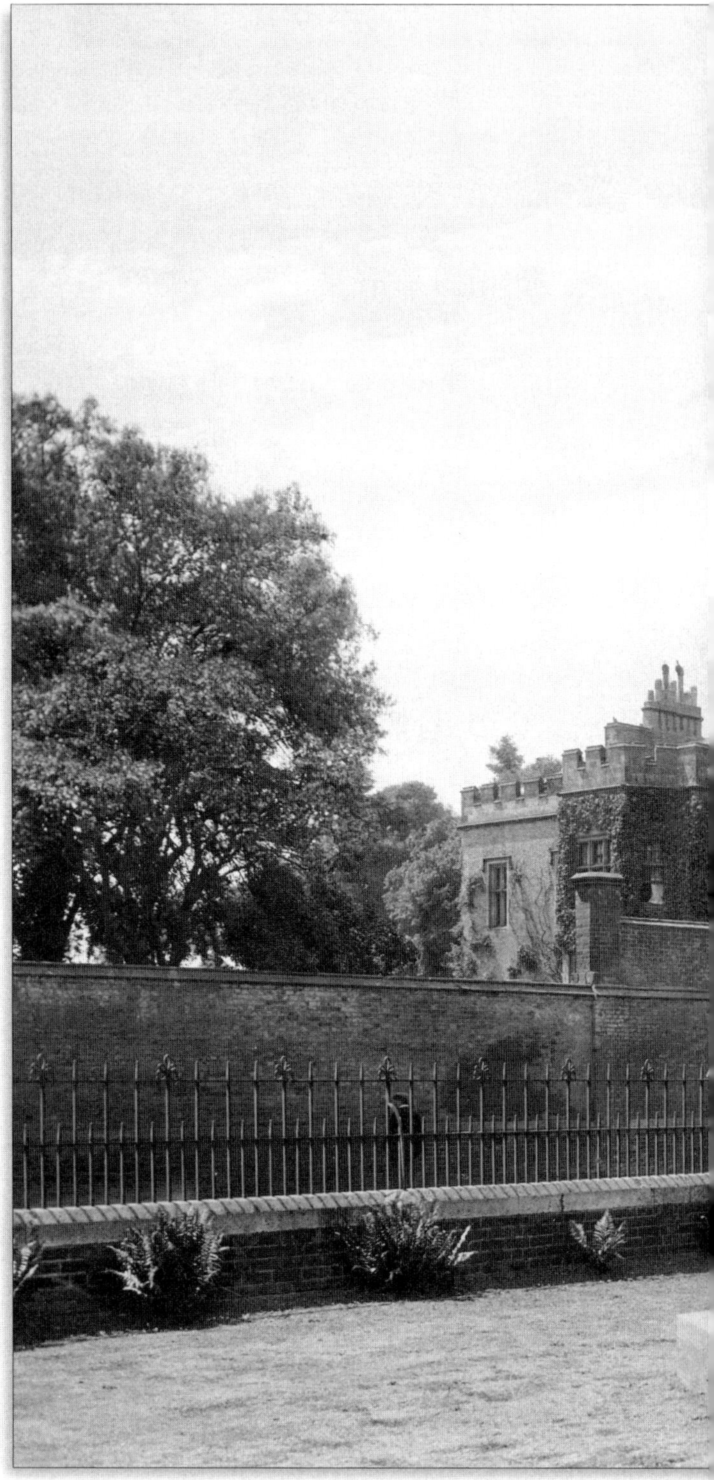

The Memorial Cross 1922 72162

The Memorial Cross stands outside the Macready Theatre. The inscription reads: 'In remembrance of our dead 1914-1919. Their names are recorded in the Memorial Chapel'.

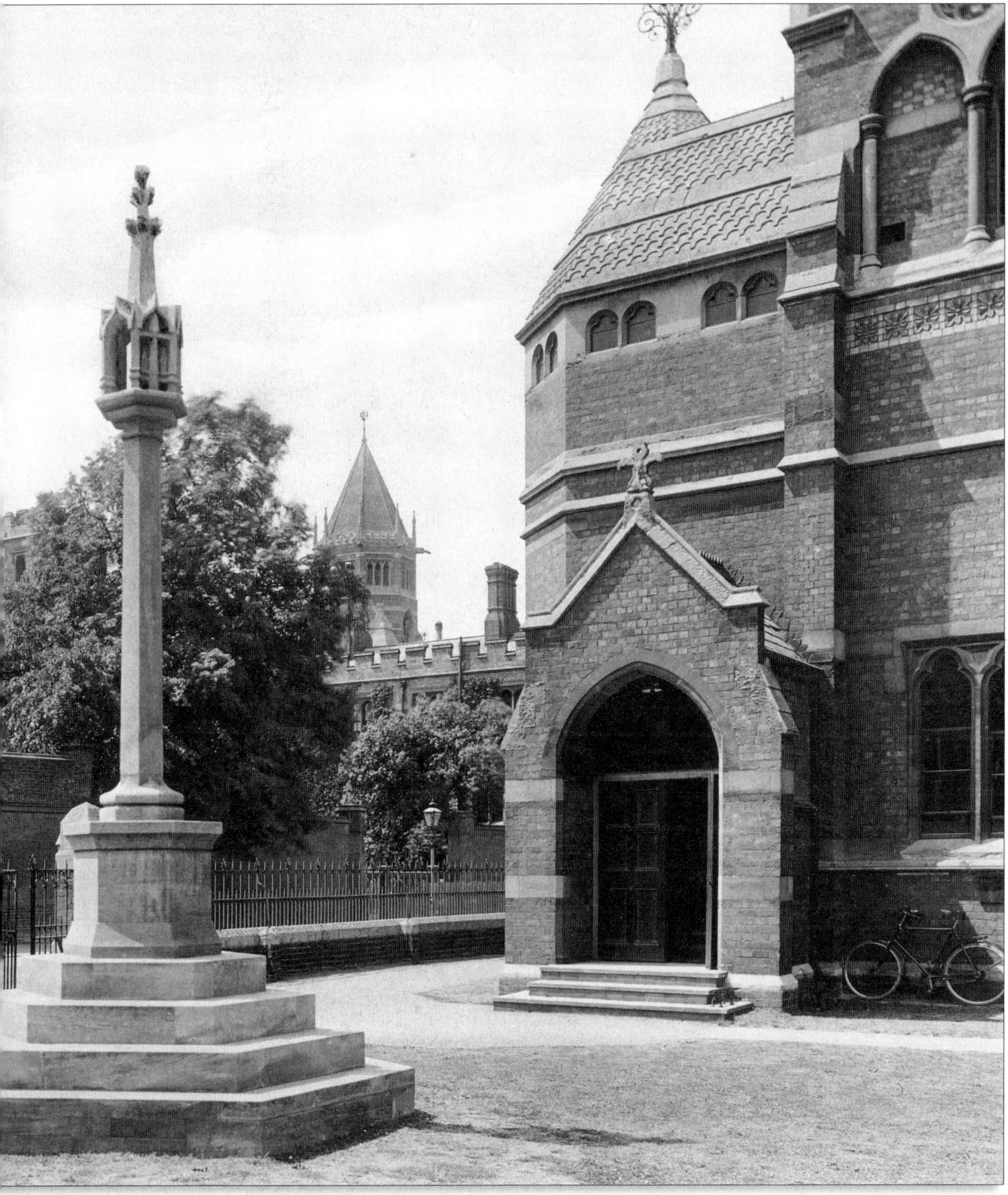

Rugby School

In 1867, £7,000 was raised by subscription and the chapel was substantially rebuilt, with the addition of a chancel and a 138 ft octagonal tower. The chapel is a particularly fine example of the polychromatic brickwork that was Butterfield's trademark, and the tower with its short spire, completed in 1882, forms a prominent local landmark (85184, page 25).

Dr Arnold obtained four ancient stained glass windows for the chapel, adding others later, some of which commemorate those Old Rugbeians who died during the Crimean War and the Indian Mutiny. Dr Arnold is the only Headmaster buried in the chapel, but there are monuments to many others, including Dr James (by Chantry), Dr Wooll (by Westmacott) and AC Tait (by Sir Edgar Boehm). Dr Arnold's memorial is by John Thomas, principal sculptor of the carved work on the Houses of Parliament.

Further extensive building at Rugby School continued into the 1880s, including New Big School, which had classrooms below and one large hall above for speeches, ceremonies and prize-giving.

The Memorial Chapel, seen from Dunchurch Road in 85186, opposite, was built in 1923. The interior walls are lined with stone tablets bearing the names of the 700 Rugbeians killed during the First World War, and the 400 killed during the Second World War. The windows were commissioned by Old Rugbeians.

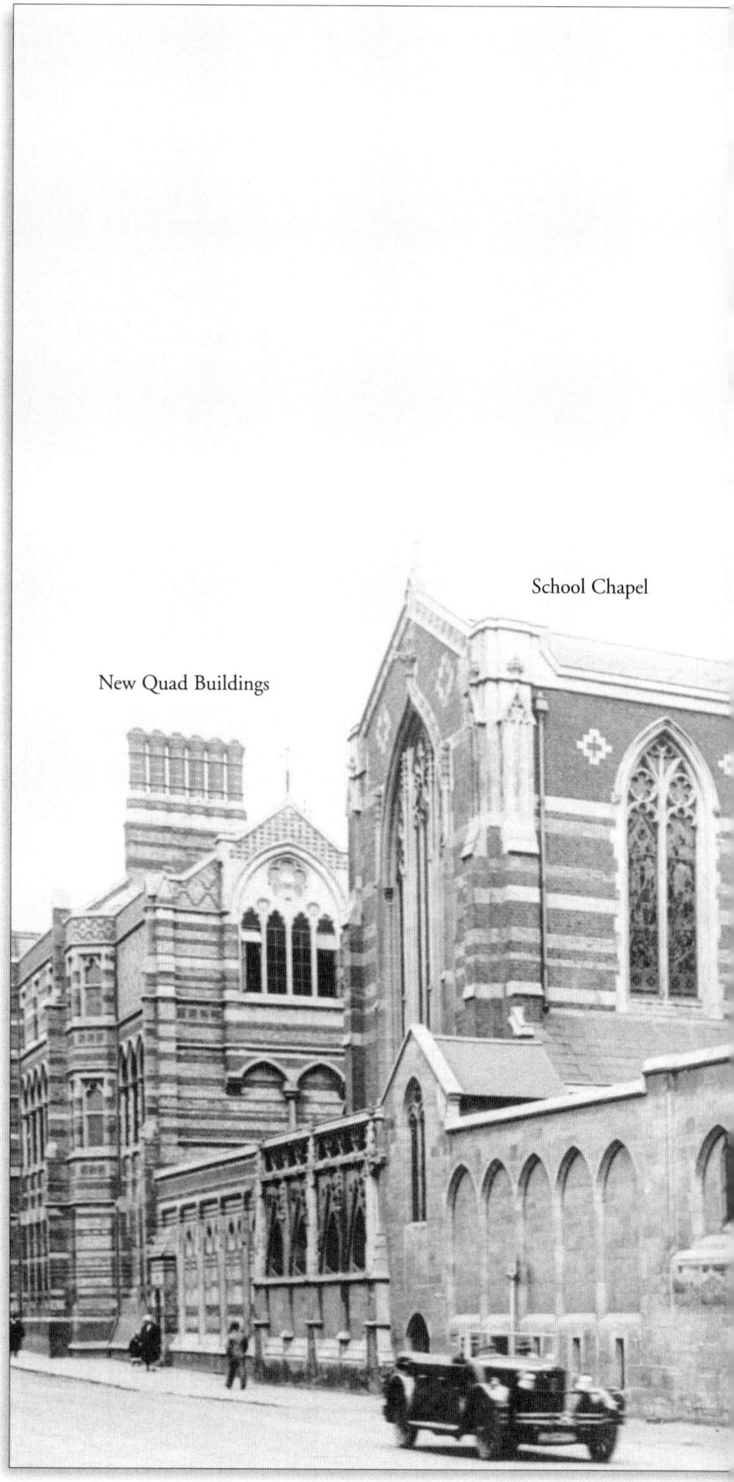

The Memorial Chapel 1932 85186

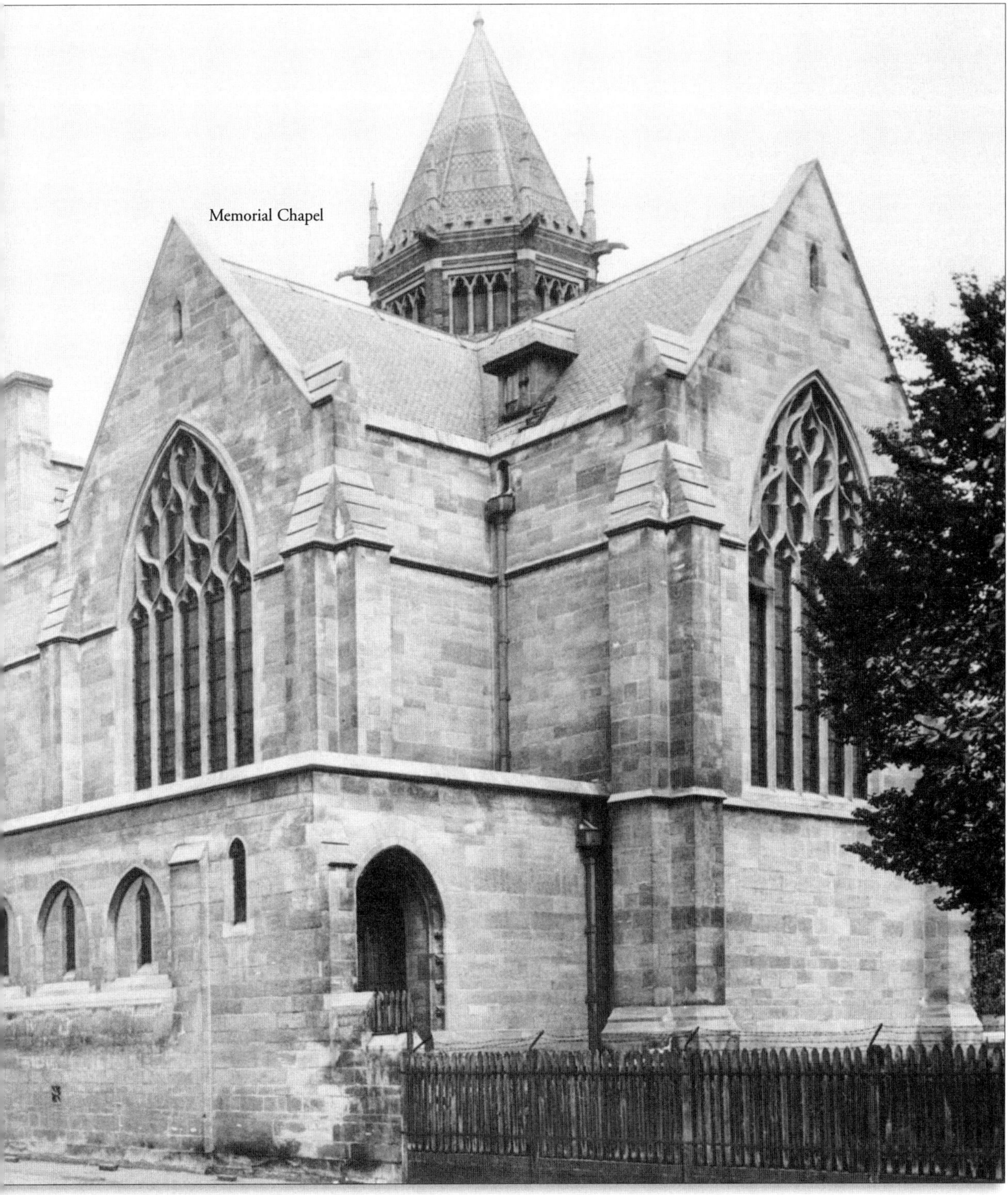

Memorial Chapel

Rugby School

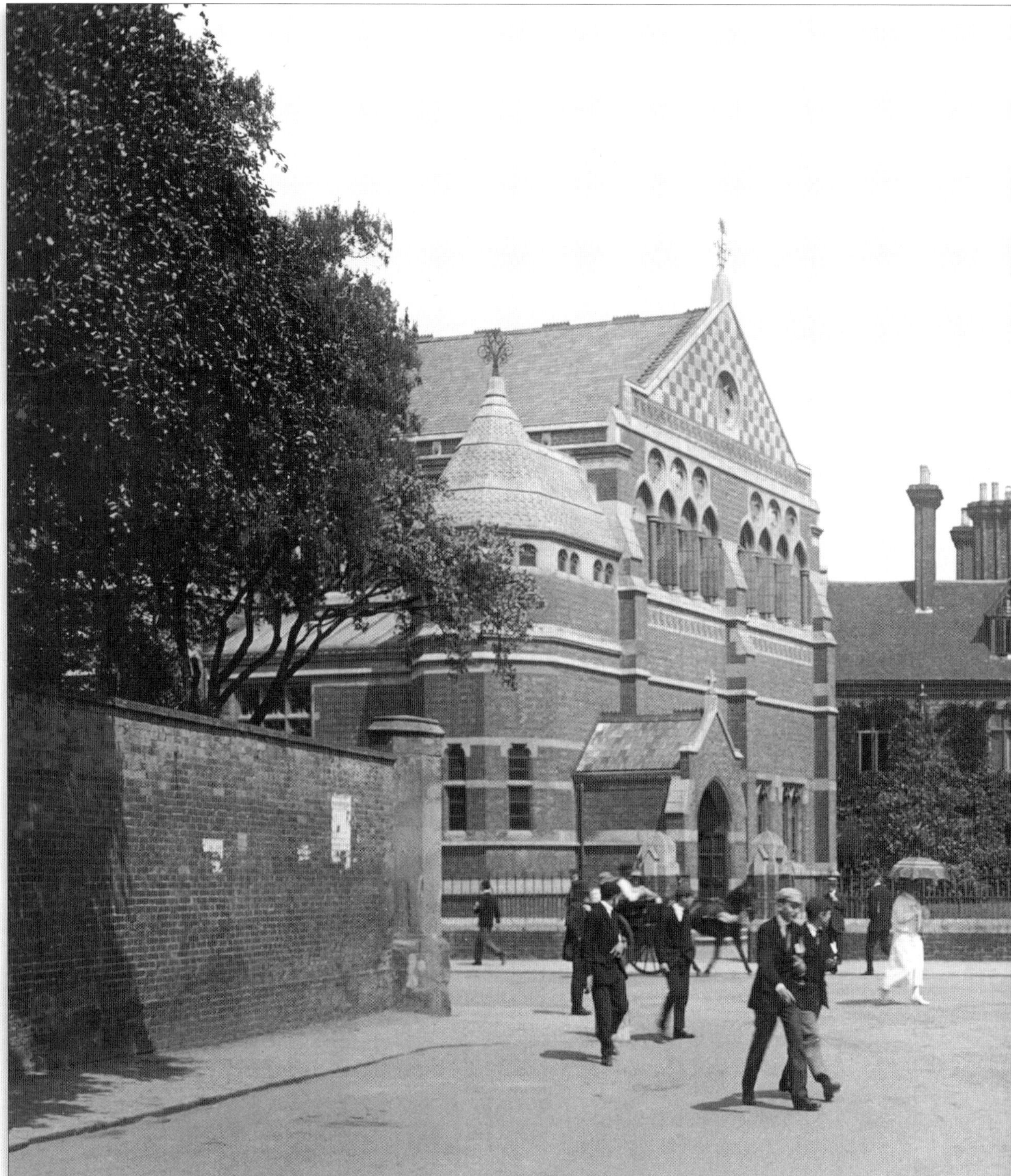

Rugby School 1922 72123

Taken from Barby Road, this photograph shows New Big School, which in the late 1970s became the Macready Theatre. Behind lies the School Museum, which was once the home of Richard and Elizabeth Wood, who founded Rugby's St Cross Hospital in 1884.

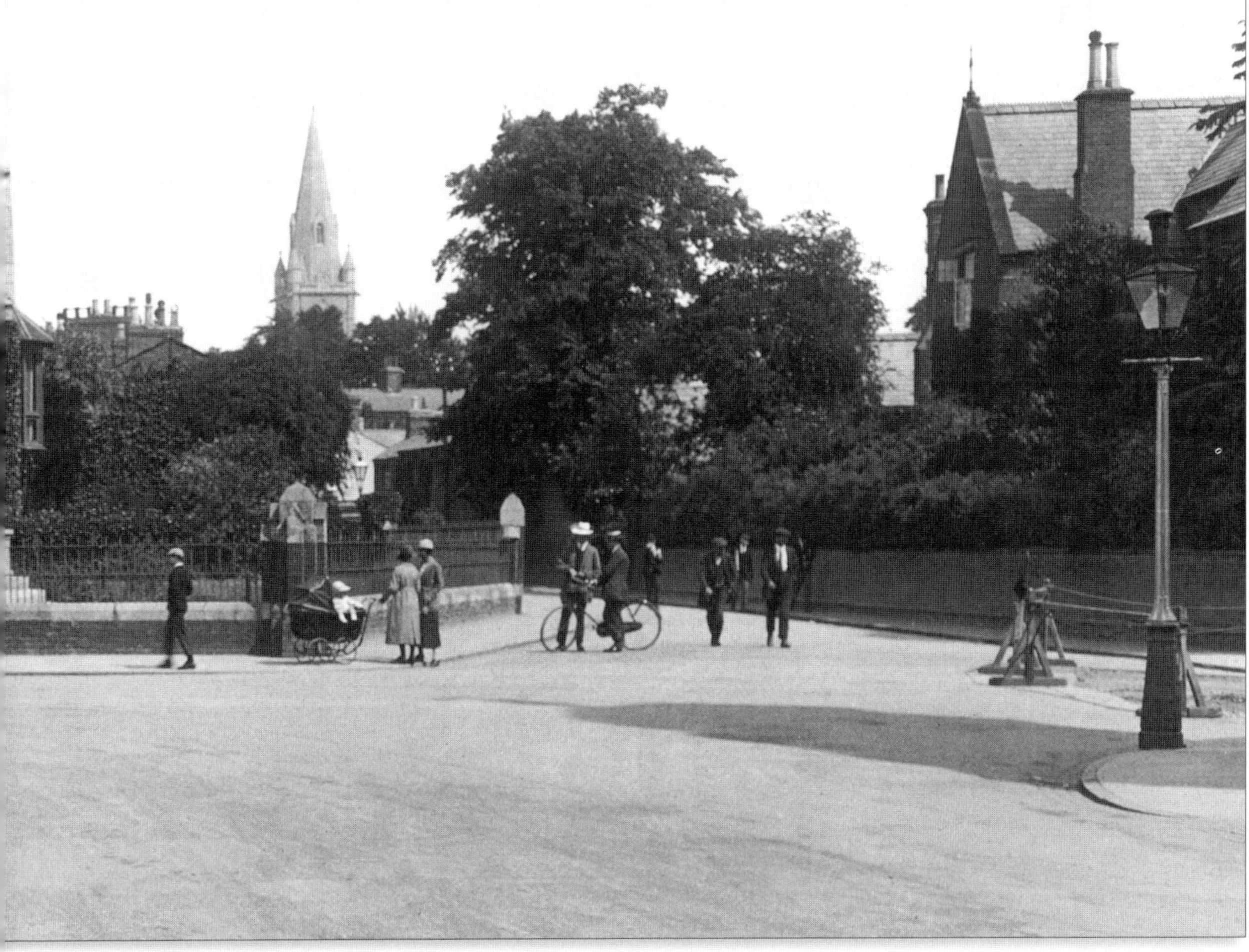

RUGBY SCHOOL

In 1997 a statue of William Webb Ellis was unveiled by the rugby player Jeremy Guscott in front of the New Quad building. On St Matthew Street opposite once lay Gilbert's Rugby Football Museum, where rugby balls had been made by hand since the first half of the 19th century. Sadly, Gilbert's has now been moved, but the connection continues since the shop, with its original 35-paned window, now houses the Rugby Museum.

Lawrence Sheriff would be amazed at his legacy today, and even more astonished to learn that in 1975 Rugby School admitted girls for the first time, and is now fully co-educational.

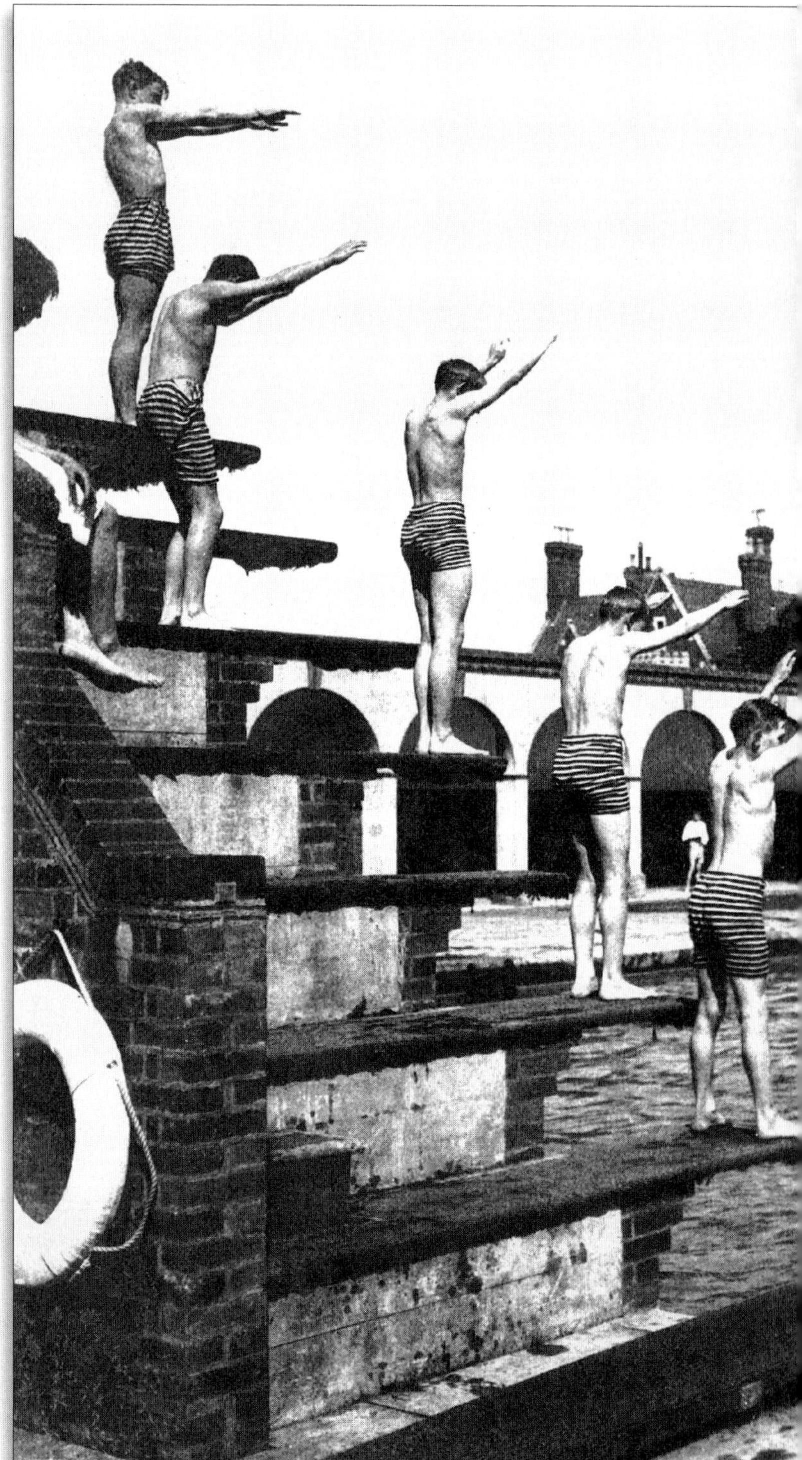

THE OPEN AIR SWIMMING BATHS 1932 85188

In 1876 the Rev Jex-Blake, Dean of Wells and ex-Headmaster of Rugby School, donated £3,000 to build a large, heated swimming pool on the Close, on the site of an old plunge-bath shed dating from 1790. These baths closed in the early 1900s, and in 1928 the baths seen here were opened off Horton Crescent. They were replaced in 1991 by the new school Sports Centre. Notice the standard school swimming trunks, known to the boys as 'bimbags'.

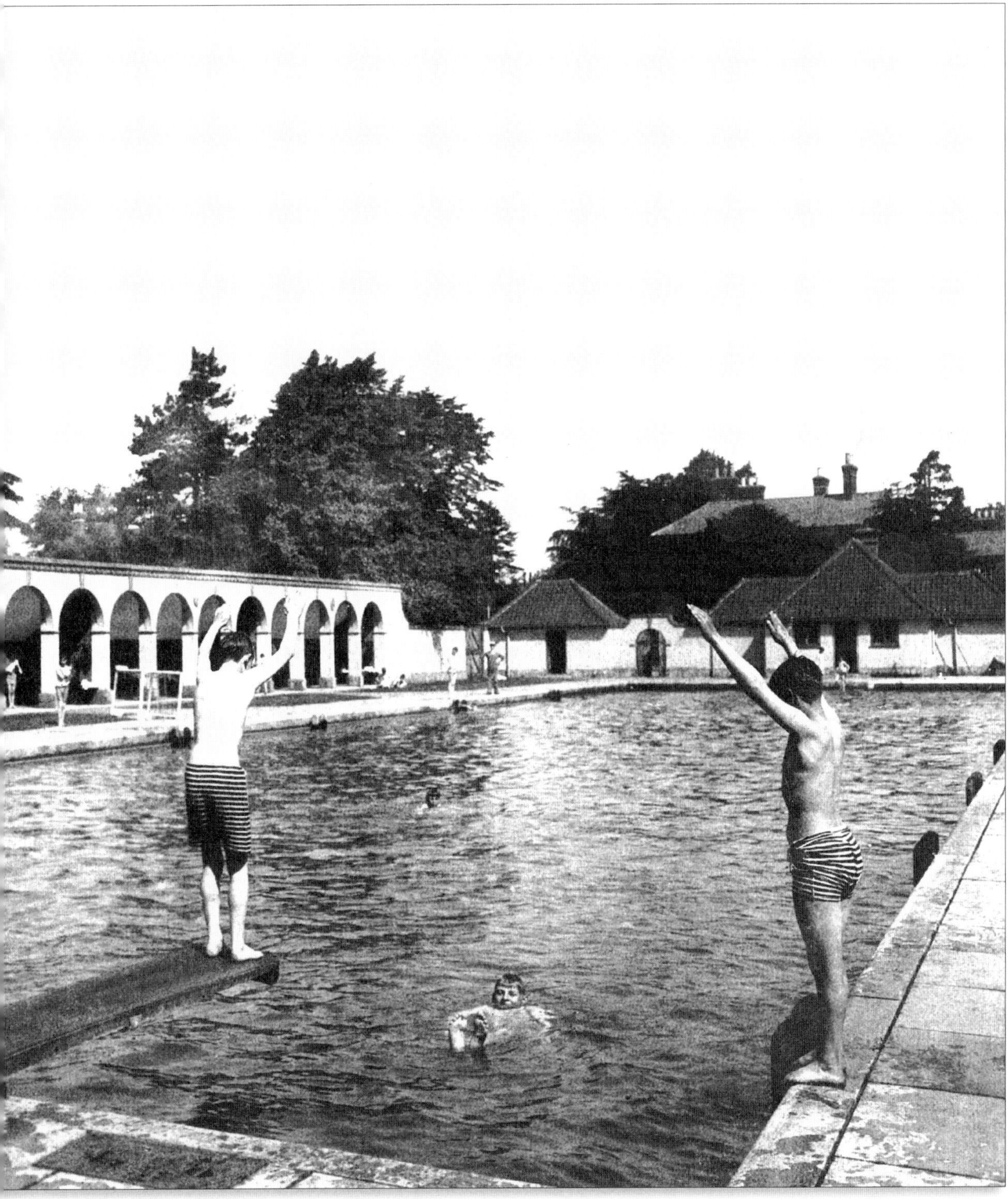

Warwickshire County Map

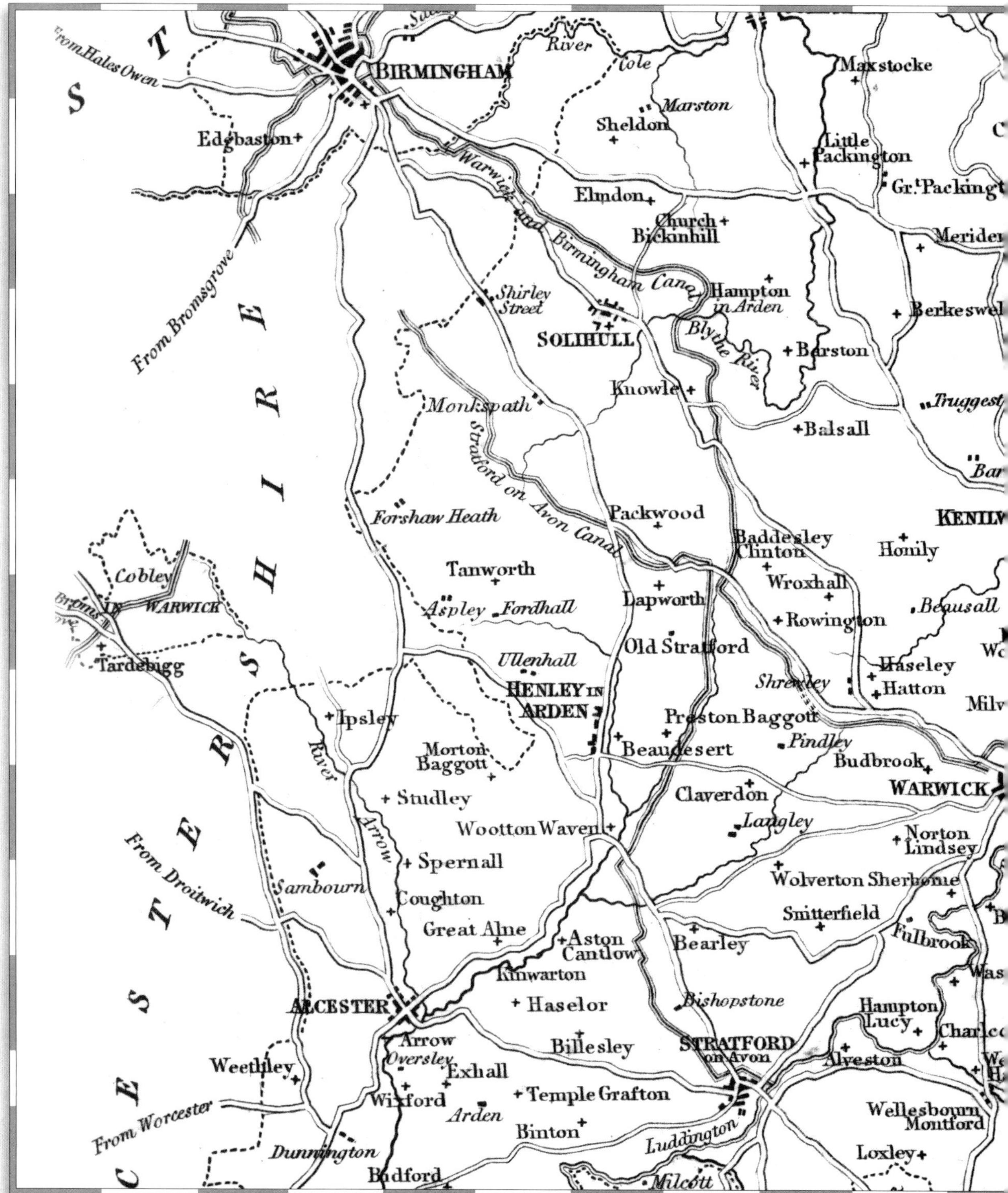

Warwickshire County Map

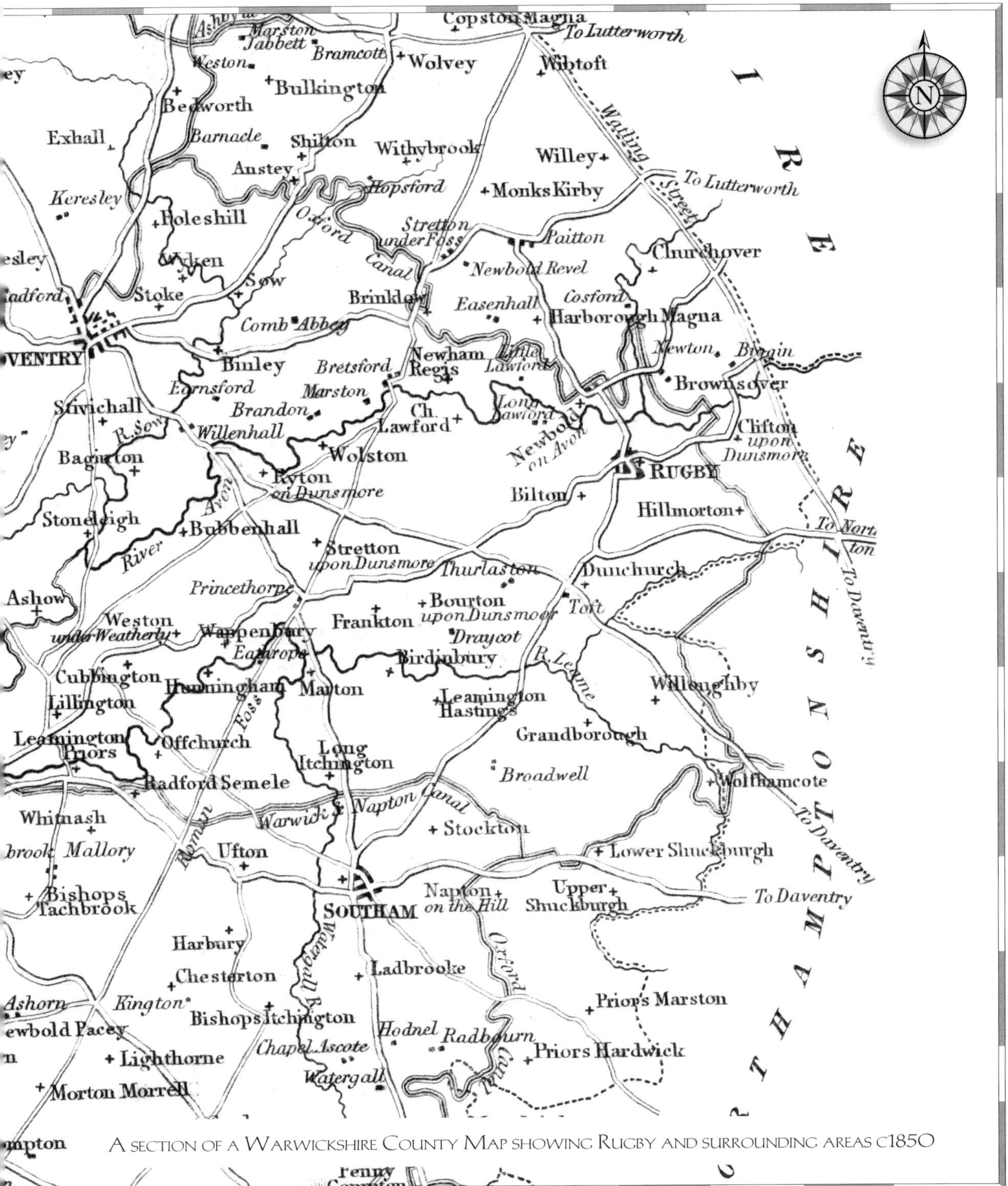

A section of a Warwickshire County Map showing Rugby and surrounding areas c1850

ST ANDREW'S AND OTHER RUGBY CHURCHES

ST ANDREW'S Parish Church is situated in Church Street, opposite the site of the original School House. There has probably been a place of worship here since Saxon times, but it was not until the 13th century that St Andrew's became Rugby's parish church.

By 1711 the church possessed five bells and a set of chimes. Until about the middle of the 19th century, the third (curfew) bell was rung daily at five in the morning and eight in the evening, warning householders to extinguish their fires until morning; this custom dates back to the time of William the Conqueror. St Andrew's is unique in having a peal of 5 bells in the mediaeval west tower and a second peal of 8 bells in the Victorian east tower.

Clifton Road, a quiet road in the 1950s, and now a busy thoroughfare, leads to the village of Clifton-on-Dunsmore. Both Rugby and Brownsover were once hamlets in the parish of Clifton, their churches merely chapels-of-ease under the mother church at Clifton-on-Dunsmore, itself attached to the Abbey of Leicester. In 1221 the Lord of the Manor, Henry de Rokeby, reached a financial arrangement with the Abbot of Leicester that effectively converted the chapel in Rugby into a parish church.

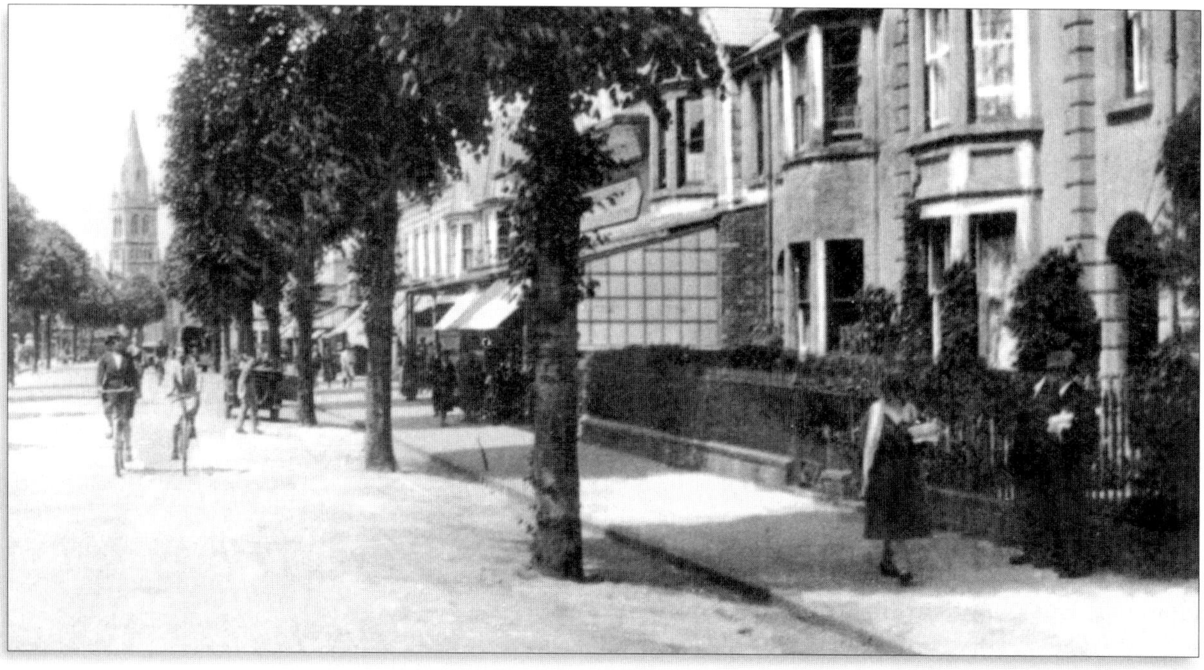

CLIFTON ROAD c1950 R69053D

ST ANDREW'S AND OTHER RUGBY CHURCHES

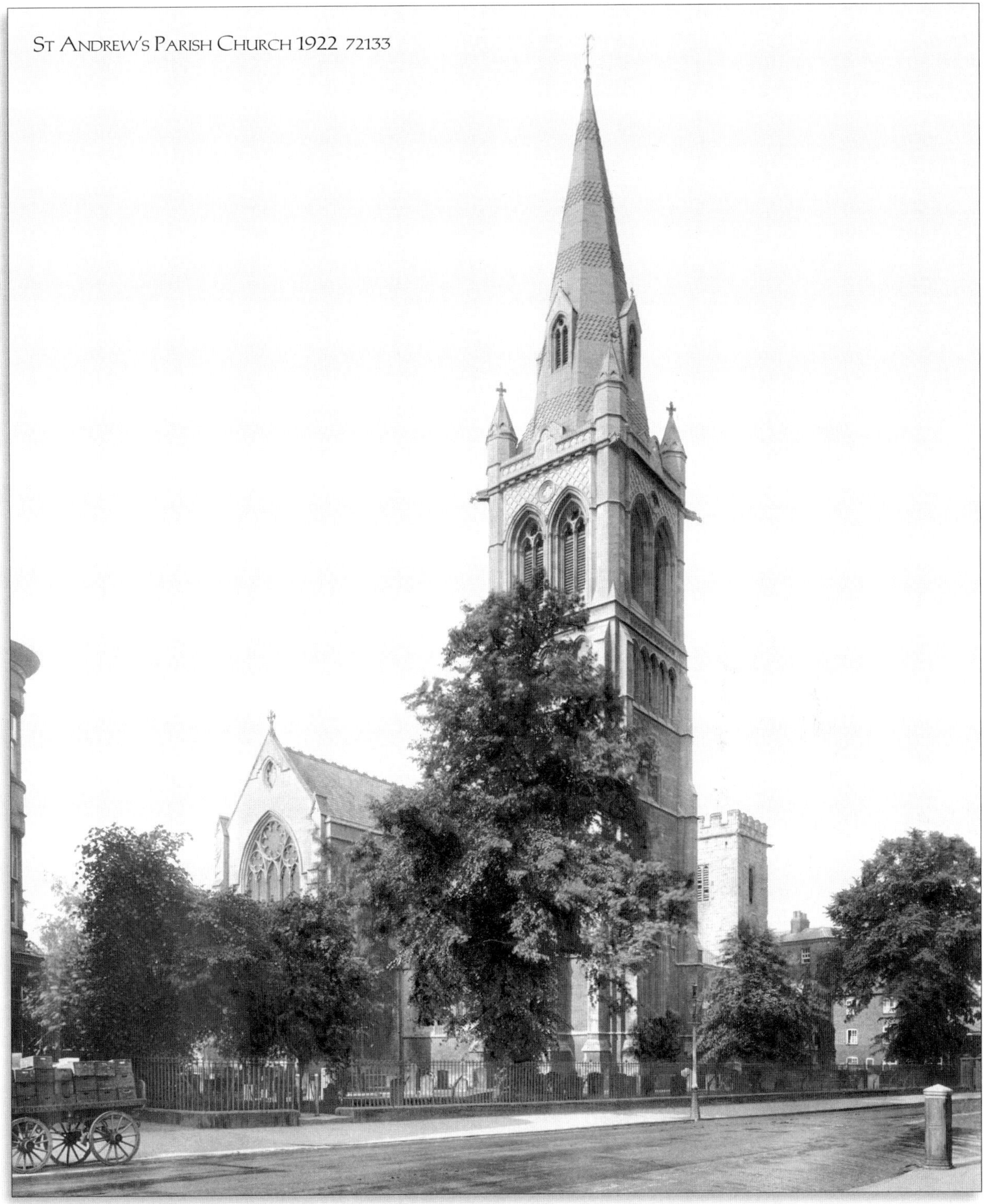

ST ANDREW'S PARISH CHURCH 1922 72133

St Andrew's and other Rugby Churches

This separation of St Andrew's Church from the Abbey of Leicester was to save its assets from seizure at the dissolution of the monasteries during the reign of Henry VIII — a fate suffered by both the church at Clifton and its remaining chapel at Brownsover. Henry de Rokeby pulled down the old Norman chancel and rebuilt it in 13th-century style, adding an unusual tower (72131, opposite): early commentators believed that it was intended as a place of defence, and that its construction was an attempt to circumvent the law forbidding the unlicensed building of fortifications.

Until 1652 the church was much neglected, but after complaints about its dangerous state it underwent extensive alteration and enlargement. However, it still failed to keep up with the rapid rise in the town's population throughout the 19th century, and the decision was made to rebuild the church entirely. The builders Parnell & Son and the architect William Butterfield were commissioned, and in 1877 the foundation stone was laid by Dr Temple, Bishop of Exeter and former headmaster of Rugby School. Costing over £20,000, the work was completed in 1880.

The font seen at the front of photograph 72137, opposite, dates from 1743. The medieval font, in which Lawrence Sheriff had been baptised, was relegated to the courtyard of the Eagle Hotel. It served as a trough for the pump until it was rescued by the Rugby historian Matthew Bloxham. It was left in the Percival Guildhouse garden behind St Matthew's Church until it was finally returned to St Andrew's in the 1950s.

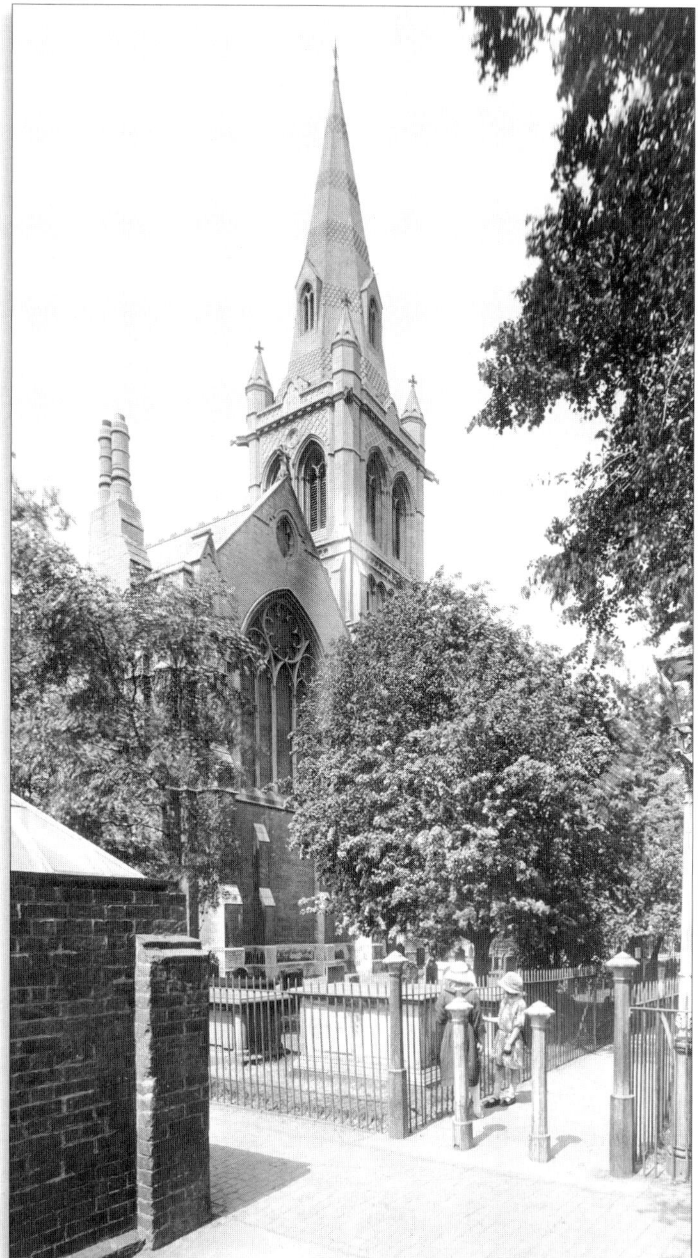

St Andrew's Parish Church 1922 72135

St Andrew's is seen here from Church Walk. The gravestones glimpsed through the railings have now been replaced by an attractive garden with benches.

St Andrew's and other Rugby Churches

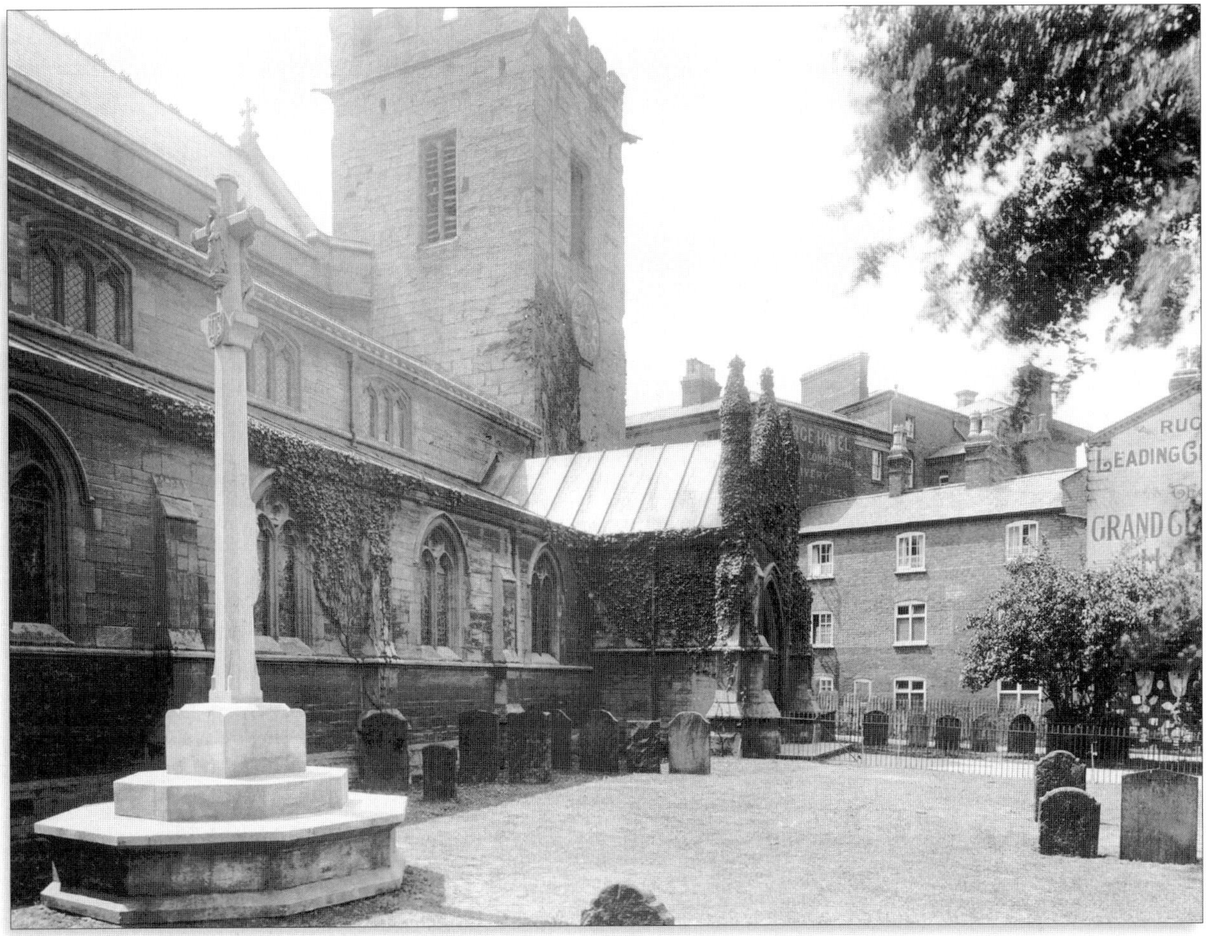

Above: St Andrew's Parish Church 1922 72131

The west tower of St Andrew's church has a distinctly castle-like appearance. Some of the building materials may have been obtained from the site of Rokeby Castle, demolished around 1157. The War Memorial is situated by the north door. The simple inscription reads: 'AD 1914-1919 1939-1945'.

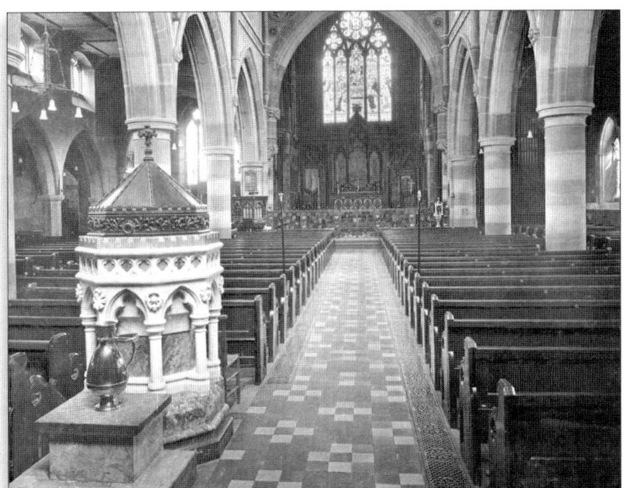

Right: The Interior of St Andrew's Parish Church 1922 72137

St Andrew's and other Rugby Churches

Throughout the 19th century, several other churches and chapels appeared, including St Matthew's, originally a chapel-of-ease to St Andrew's. St Matthew's (R69052D, below) was intended to serve the western side of the town, where new streets and houses were rapidly springing up: it is situated on the corner of Elborow Street (now Bloxham Place) and Warwick Road (now Warwick Street, part of the gyratory system dating from 1980). The church was built in 1841 with money raised by private subscription, on land donated by Dr R Bloxham, father of Matthew Bloxham. Designed by Mr Hussey of Birmingham in the Early English style of the 13th century, it was built at a cost of £2,849 by Mr Lockington of Rugby. The external facing was of Yorkshire stone, and the roof was of slate. The original bell, housed in the bell turret in the west gable, was made by Mr J Sneath.

Box pews were originally installed in St Matthew's, their quarterly rentals ranging from 4s (first class) to 1s 6d (fourth class). These pews were replaced in 1902, but the pew rents continued until 1920. The chancel was added to the church in 1912, and the rare and lovely east window above the reredos is made of pure colour glass. In 1874 St Matthew's became a parish church in its own right, but long before that time a second chapel-of-ease had been required for St Andrew's, a need met in 1854 by the building of Holy Trinity Church (72132, pages 46-47).

Holy Trinity was designed by Sir George Gilbert Scott in the Decorated Gothic style. It was originally intended to have a spire, but the foundations proved too weak. The finished church was in a cruciform shape with a central tower. In 1883 the tower was seen to be cracking,

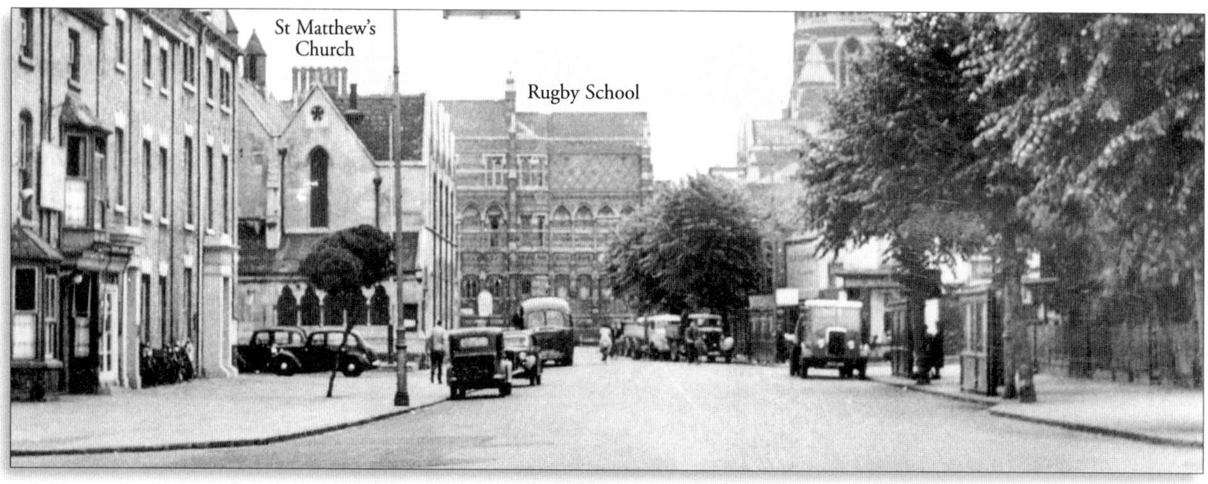

WARWICK STREET C1950 R69052D

Originally, St Matthew's Church (left) contained just two side aisles and a nave. Subsequent widening of the aisles, and the addition of galleries on each side and at the west end, provided seating for 1,000 — more than any other church in Rugby. Later alterations substantially reduced this seating capacity. Addison Row (far left) was built during the 1840s in the distinctive yellow brick extensively used in Rugby during the 1800s. The small front gardens had disappeared by the 1950s, and have been replaced today by a raised flowerbed along the pavement edge. The William Webb Ellis public house now occupies the left-hand end of the row.

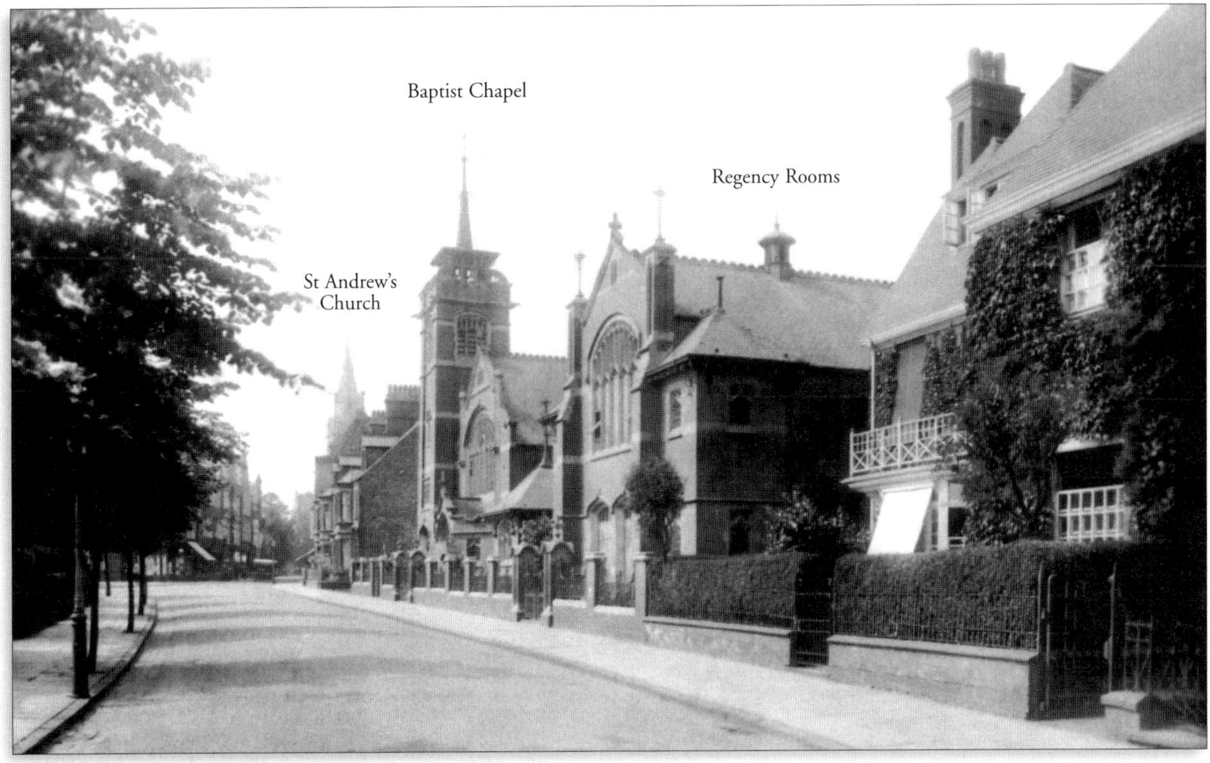

THE BAPTIST CHAPEL, REGENT PLACE 1922 72118

Here we see the Baptist Chapel (centre), with the Regency Rooms to the right. From 1910 to 1973 the town's public baths were to be found to the far left of this photograph, out of camera shot. They were replaced by the small Jubilee Gardens created in 1973 to commemorate the Silver Jubilee of Queen Elizabeth II. Here, in 1988, was unveiled a statue of the famous Rugby poet and Old Rugbeian, Rupert Brooke, who died in 1915 aged 28. The Jubilee Gardens are believed to stand on the site of both a Bronze Age tumulus and the original Celtic hill-fort or settlement of Rugby.

and was underpinned with concrete. The architect, C F Bodley, who was called in after the death of Scott, also advised on the replacing of the piers and arches on the west side with a stronger stone, and removing the pinnacle from the north-west corner of the tower. Mr Bodley went on to design the chancel screen, the outer case of the organ and the east window, which was dedicated to the memory of the Rev J Moultrie.

Several other denominations were catered for in Rugby during the 19th century, including the Congregationalists, who in 1865 were obliged to worship in the Town Hall. As the congregation grew, however, a site was found in Albert Street for a permanent place of worship. This church was opened in 1867.

Rugby's first Baptist chapel was built in 1803 by Sir Egerton Leigh, who was minister there until 1811. Situated in Regent Place, this chapel was rebuilt and enlarged in 1881.

The Methodists held their first services in Rugby in a cottage in Riley's Court (off Dunchurch Road), and

St Andrew's and other Rugby Churches

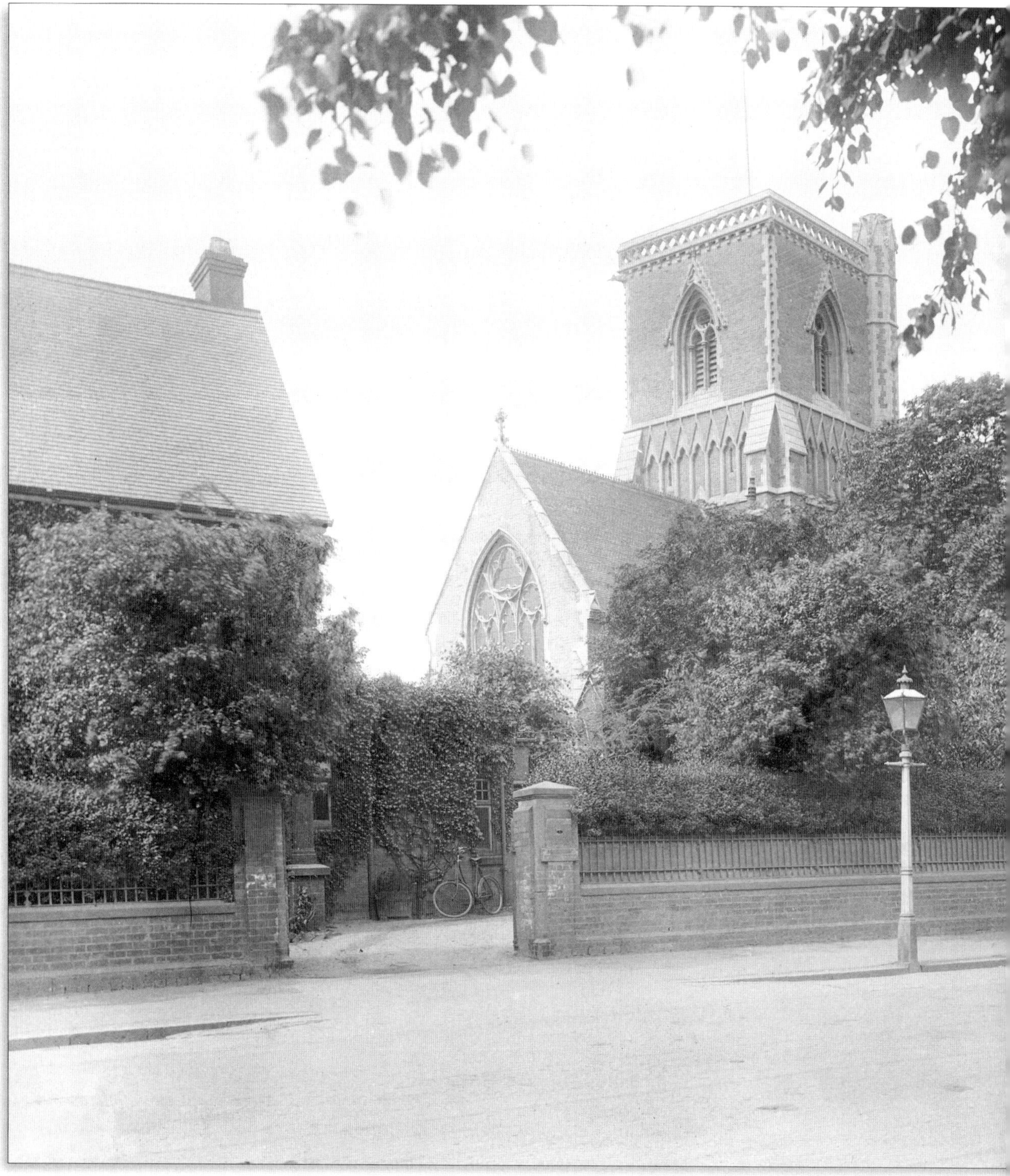

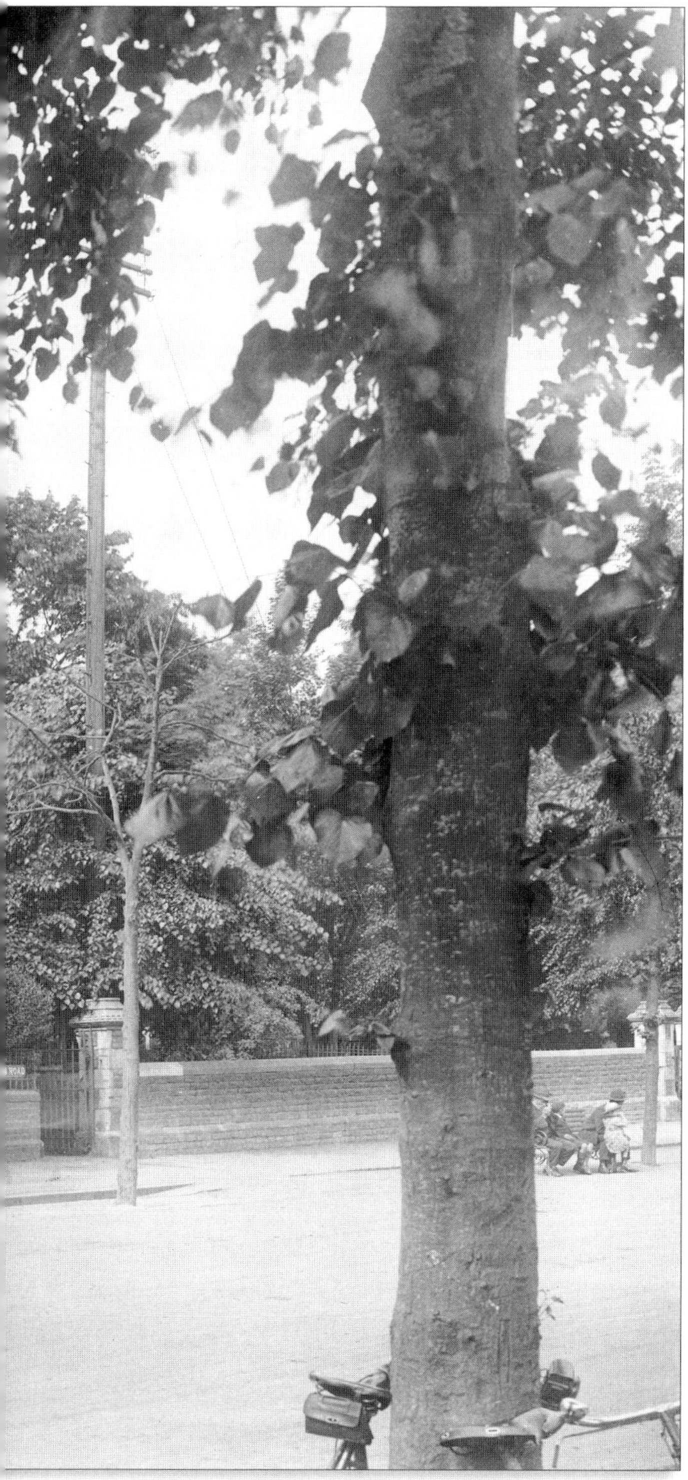

not long afterwards constructed a small chapel in Harral's Court, off Drury Lane. In 1823 a larger chapel, holding a congregation of 400, was built in Chapel Street (formerly Swan Street). A new chapel, capable of accommodating 600, was opened in Market Place in 1869, and in 1883 a small additional chapel was built in Cambridge Street at a cost of £800. A greengrocer's shop now stands on the site of the Market Place chapel, which was demolished in 1980; its replacement was built on Russelheim Way.

In 1841 the Primitive Methodists built a small chapel on the corner of Queen Street and Russell Street, but in 1877 they moved to a far larger chapel in Railway Terrace. This imposing structure of red brick and stone was designed by Mr Kerridge and built at a cost of £2,175.

The prettiest church in Rugby is St Marie's Catholic Church (R69019, page 48), built in 1848 by Captain J H Washington-Hibbert for his Catholic wife, Julia. The church was designed by Augustus Welby Pugin, who also designed Birmingham Catholic Cathedral and, in conjunction with Sir Charles Barry, the Houses of Parliament.

HOLY TRINITY CHURCH 1922 72132

Holy Trinity Church eventually went out of use. It was damaged by fire in 1980 and was finally demolished in 1983, when a new rectory and Trinity Court retirement flats were built on the site. The old churchyard provides a pleasant pathway from the old lych gate on Church Street (where it becomes Clifton Road) to Little Church Street.

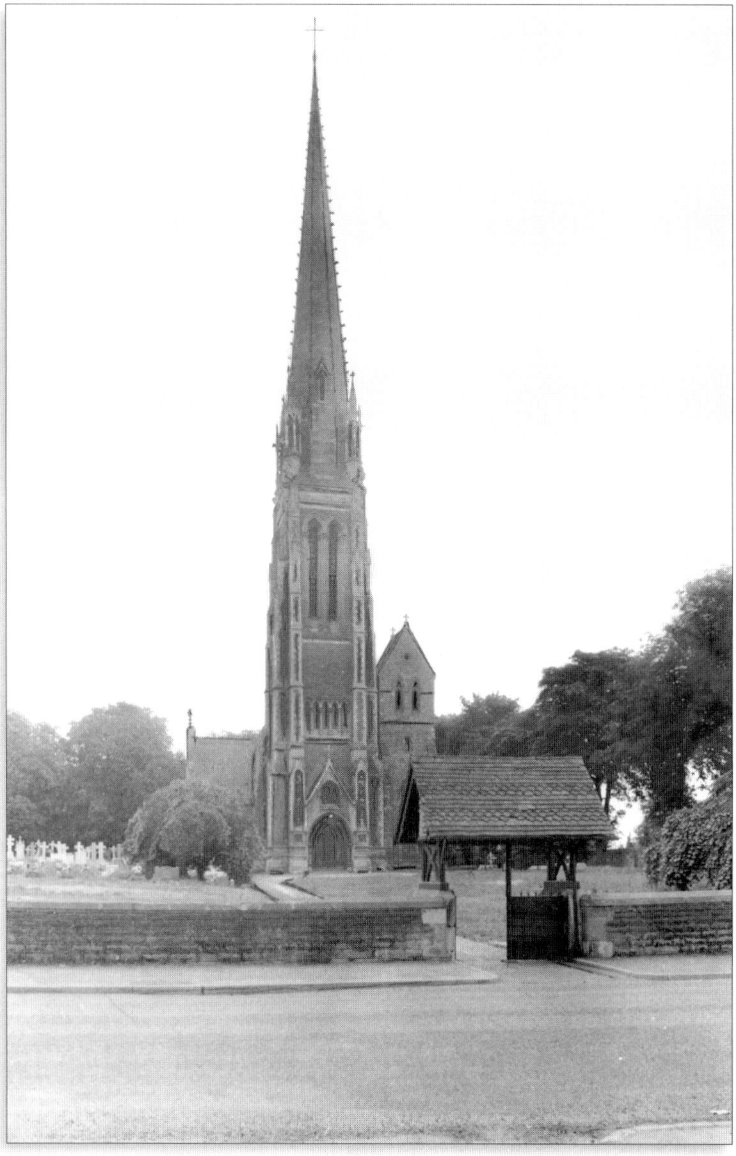

ST MARIE'S CHURCH C1955 R69019

Situated on Dunchurch Road, St Marie's was Rugby's first Catholic church. The 200ft spire is of the Early Gothic style of the 14th century, and was designed by Mr B Whelan of London. Its metal gilt cross was surmounted originally by a cockerel — a symbol of Christian wakefulness. The small square Norman-style tower contains a peal of 8 large bells manufactured by Mears of Whitechapel.

In 1862 the church was enlarged, with a spacious nave replacing the original aisle and Lady Chapel, leaving the nave and chancel to form the south aisle. Unfortunately the tiny saddleback tower of the old church was now seriously out of proportion to the new, larger church. Captain Hibbert, now a Catholic convert, paid for a new spire and tower, both of which were constructed of Ancaster stone with ashlar dressings of the same material; the sculpture was mainly of Portland stone. The interior work was carried out by Parnell & Son.

John Hardman of Birmingham made many of St Marie's stained glass windows, though two splendid windows in the south aisle were made by Mayor of Munich. In the south aisle chapel are the archangel windows, installed in 1997 by Aidan McRae Thomson. These depict the vision of St Hubert, a hunter converted to Christianity after seeing a vision of the Holy Cross between a stag's antlers. There is a superb sculpture of St Hubert and the stag outside the west door.

Other features of interest include the wooden-beamed mediaeval style roof, the fine organ loft overhanging the west end of the church, the huge crucifix hanging above the ornate marble altar and the floor of the south aisle chapel, tiled in the Arts and Crafts style of William Morris.

BRABNER'S GAZETTEER OF ENGLAND AND WALES 1895

'Rugby, a market town, the head of a poor-law union, petty sessional division, and county court district, and a parish in Warwickshire. The town stands near the river Avon and the Oxford canal, 3 miles W of Watling Street, on the Warwickshire boundary, 5½ SE of the Fosse Way, 11½ E by S of Coventry, 15 NE of Leamington, 29½ ESE of Birmingham, and 82½ from London ... Rugby came into prominent notice in the 18th century in connection with a great grammar school founded at it in 1567, and acquired increasing importance from its position in reference to railways after the railway period.'

MARKET PLACE AND THE TOWN CENTRE

THE 12th century saw a rapid growth in trade throughout England, and an urgent need for new markets. In 1255 Henry de Rokeby bought the franchise of Rugby's Saturday market, with the right to hold a three-day fair each August.

The medieval market-place, situated at the intersection of the ancient roadways linking Leicester to Oxford and Northampton to Coventry, was simply a large triangle of open ground containing a 'shambles', where livestock were slaughtered and stalls set up for the sale of meat. There would have been a wooden cross, originating from the preaching crosses of the early Christian missionaries, for whom a crowded market provided an ideal place to preach the Gospel. In the 16th century the wooden cross was replaced by one of stone.

By the 14th century the Shambles had become a row of 12 single-storied shops with thatched roofs and half-timbered walls infilled with wattle-and-daub. Slaughtering yards lay behind the shops, and nearby stood the stocks, the pillory and the lock-up. Scolds, troublemakers and women brewers found guilty of watering their ale were sent to the ducking stool at the Horsepool on the eastern side of the town, an area now known as The Plaisance. St Andrew's (Caldecott) School was built here in 1830 after the Horsepool was filled in, but it was demolished in 1953.

By the 19th century, the Shambles had become a row of dilapidated open sheds. They were replaced in 1830 by a row of shops, officially known as Manor Buildings, each valued at £5 per annum. A two-storey section was added in about 1890.

Duke's Jetty, a small link road between Sheep Street and High Street, is a reminder of a grocery and ironmongery business that traded here from 1886 but which was replaced by a modern block in 1956.

By the 16th century, building had begun southwards from the Shambles (behind Briggs & Company, 85179), eventually forming the present High Street. The west side of Market Place was filled in during the 18th century to create Sheep Street on the east and Stockwell Lane, now Drury Lane, on the west. By the middle of the 19th century, in addition to the Saturday market there

Market Place and the Town Centre

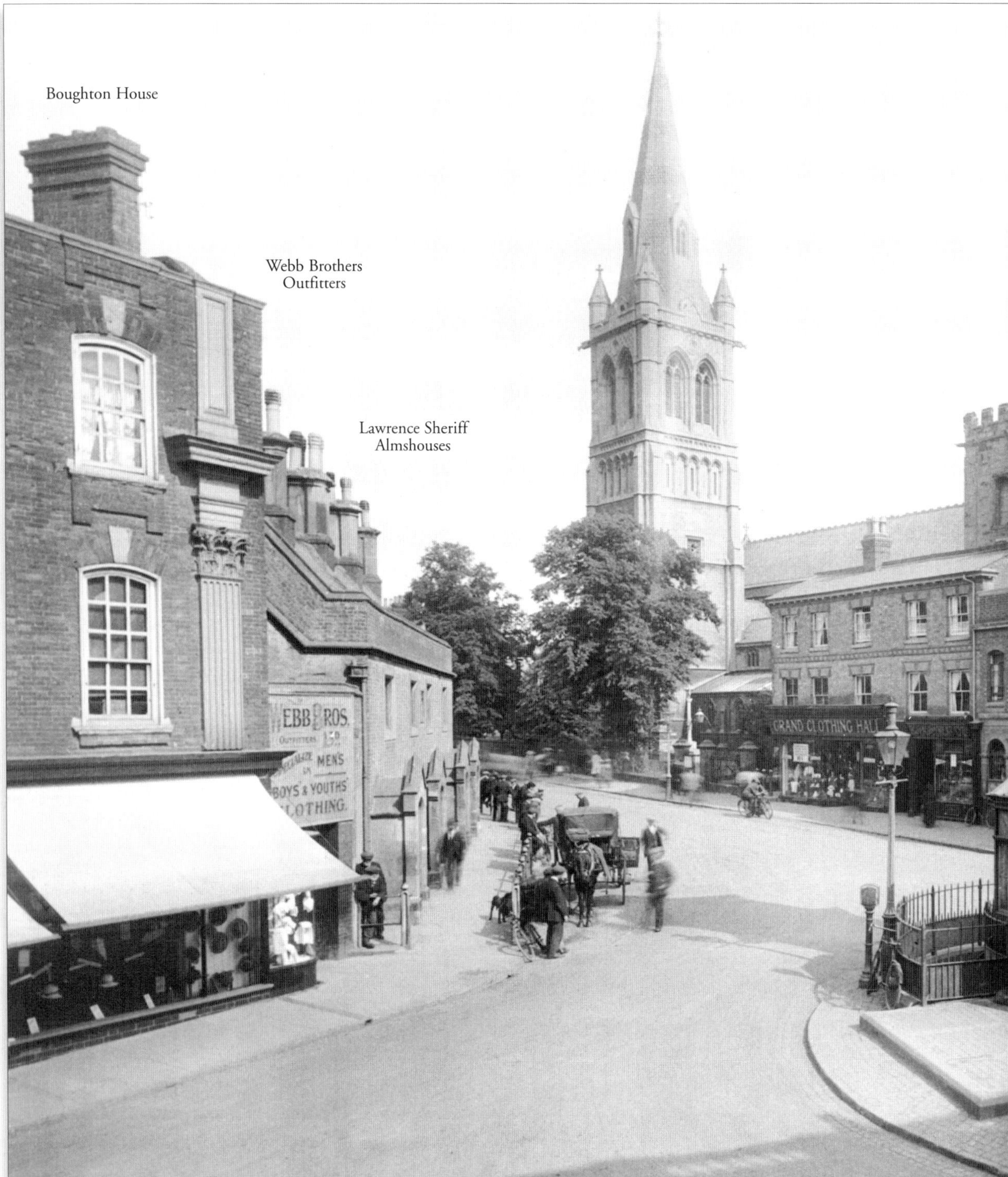

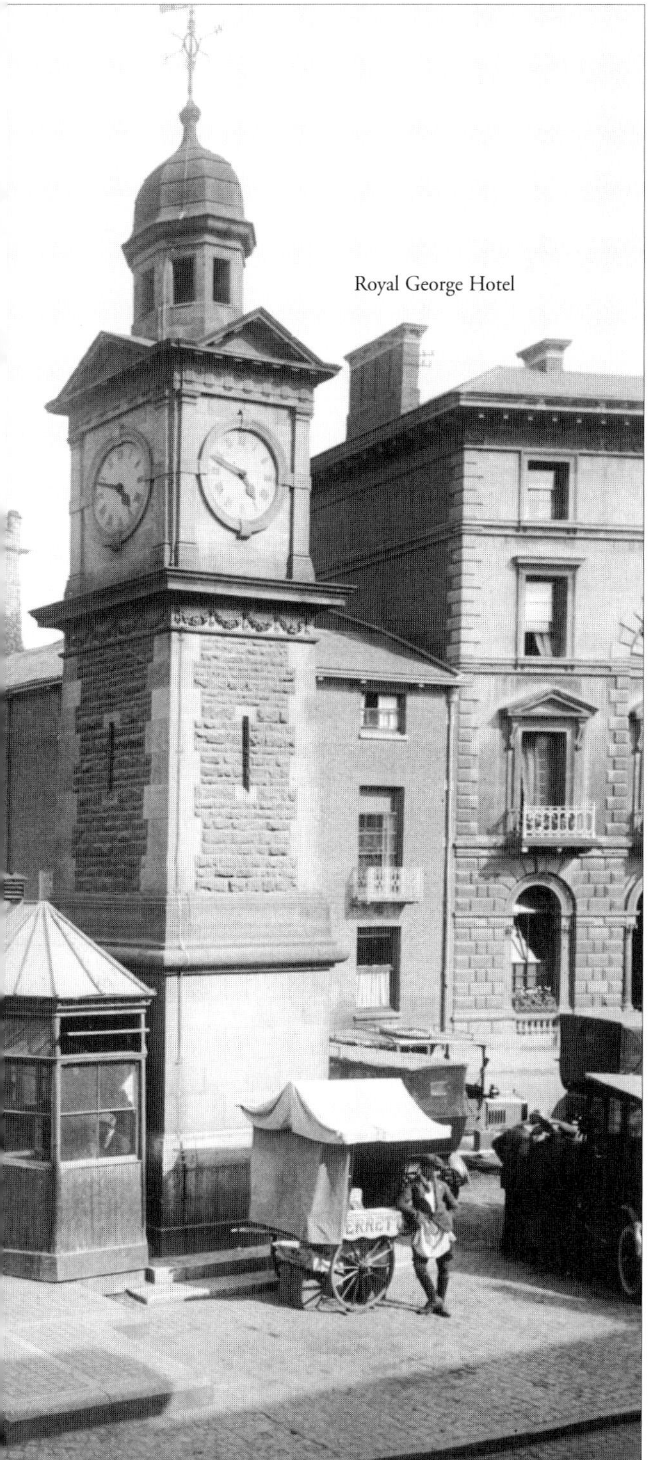

Royal George Hotel

were some 13 horse and cattle sales each year, a large Martinmas horse fair, 3 hiring fairs and 2 cheese fairs.

These fairs, the cattle markets in particular, caused almost unendurable noise, filth, stench and confusion. Horses were tied up in the streets, often to the churchyard wall; sheep and pigs were penned in the main streets; and cattle roamed everywhere, causing inconvenience and danger.

Filthy streets were not the only problem. The 15 inns in and around the Market Square provided ale at 10d a gallon and Jamaica rum at 1s 4d a bottle. Gin was even cheaper, and the unsanitary but cheap lodging houses were full of 'beggars and low Irish'. Brawling, drunkenness, singing and shouting made life almost intolerable for the respectable townsfolk. The first attempt to solve the problem was the creation of the Town Hall Company, a private organisation of wealthy townspeople, which in 1857 built Rugby's first Town Hall.

THE CLOCK TOWER AND ST ANDREW'S CHURCH 1922 72125

In 1876 the George Inn, built in 1652, was demolished to make way for the George Hotel, called the Royal George Hotel after Princess Mary, daughter of George III, stayed there (right). The hotel closed in 1951 and was demolished in 1953 to make way for a very dull row of shops. Boughton House (left, with the classical detailing), built in 1729 as a private residence, was sold in 1902 to Webb Bros. When Webb Bros closed in 1953, this beautiful house was destroyed to make way for yet another featureless row of shops. To the right of Webb Bros lie the Lawrence Sheriff Almshouses, demolished in 1961. New almshouses were built on Warwick Street. At the base of the clock tower stands a wooden cabmen's shelter.

Market Place and the Town Centre

Between the shops on the right of 85178 (page 56) lies a narrow tunnel leading into Windsor Court. In the 19th century the court housed a brewery, a malt-house store and a factory producing Windsor chairs. When the High Street was built up, a tunnel was created to maintain access to the court, which has now been opened up onto Little Church Street at the back.

Notice the extensive use of sun awnings in the photographs of the town centre. In Victorian times these were supported by poles held in sockets at the edge of the pavements. Some of these socket holes survived into the inter-war period, and were mistakenly believed to have been cattle pen stanchions.

The Town Hall housed the Council offices, the Sessions Court, the Assembly Room and the Market Hall/Corn Exchange. The butchers and farmers who attended the cheese fairs now had to set up their stalls in the Market Hall rather than in the street. In 1866 all the hiring fairs were abolished. In 1870 the cattle market was moved to the Glebe Field near Holy Trinity Church. In 1874 it moved again, to Reynolds Field, off Hillmorton Road, and in 1878 it moved yet again, to the bottom of Railway Terrace and Murray Road. No longer in use, the site is to be sold for redevelopment.

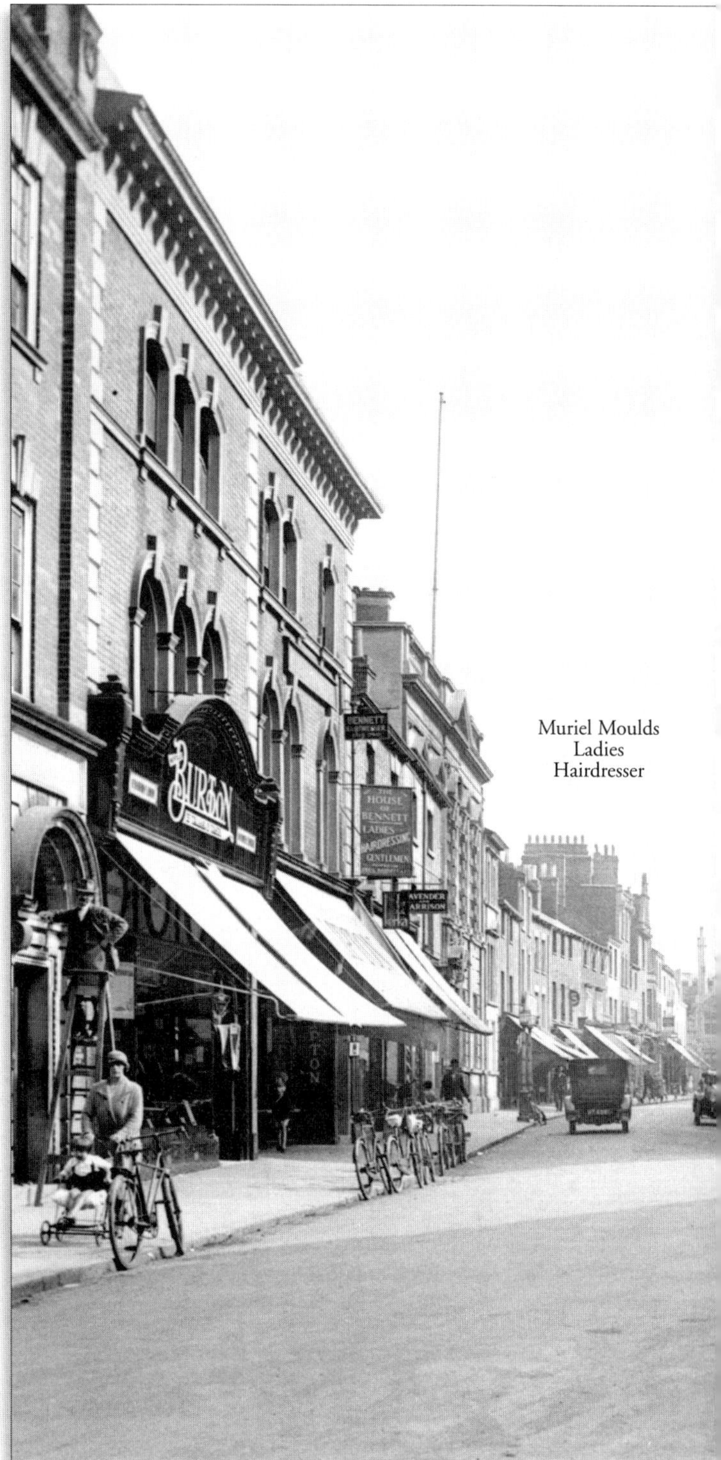

Market Place, High Street and Sheep Street 1932 85179

Briggs & Company (Peter Briggs today) has traded on this site for over a century. Durrant, a piano retailer, had previously held the site, one of at least 3 piano retailers in the town centre at the end of the 19th century. Today there are none.

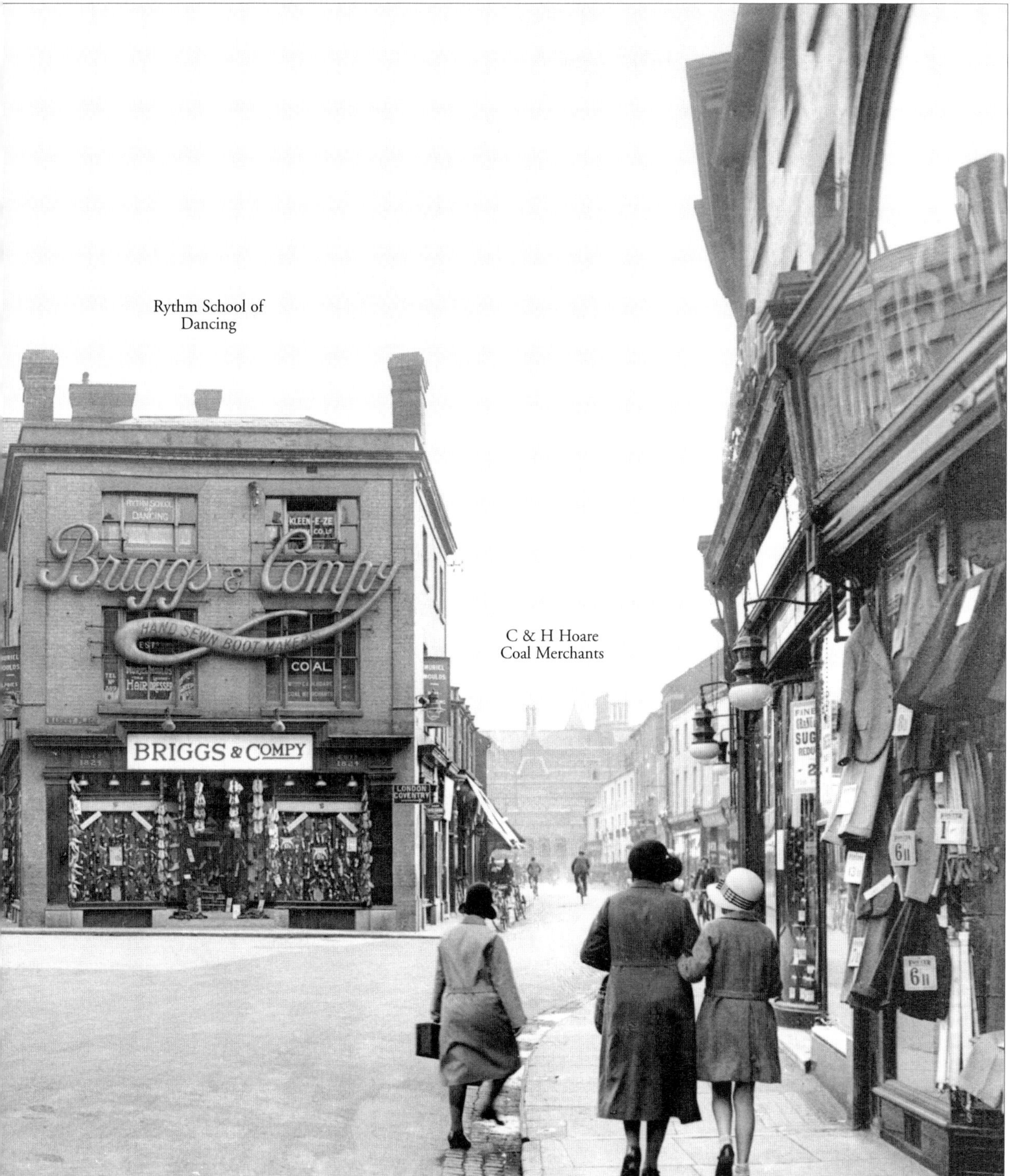
Rythm School of
Dancing
C & H Hoare
Coal Merchants
Briggs & Compy
HAND SEWN BOOT MAKER
KLEEN-E-ZE
COAL
HAIR DRESSER
BRIGGS & COMPY
LONDON
COVENTRY

Market Place and the Town Centre

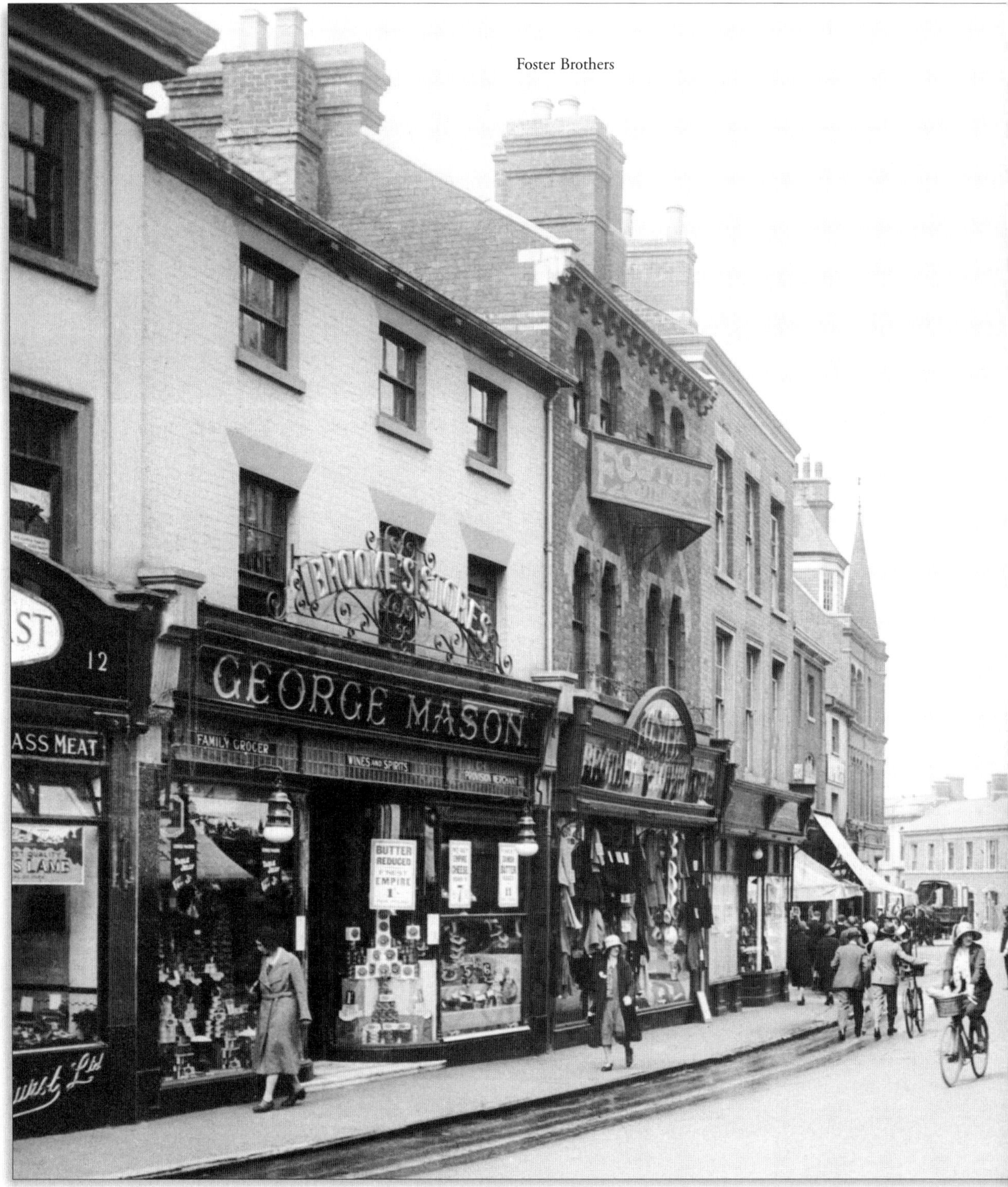

Foster Brothers

MARKET PLACE 1932 85177

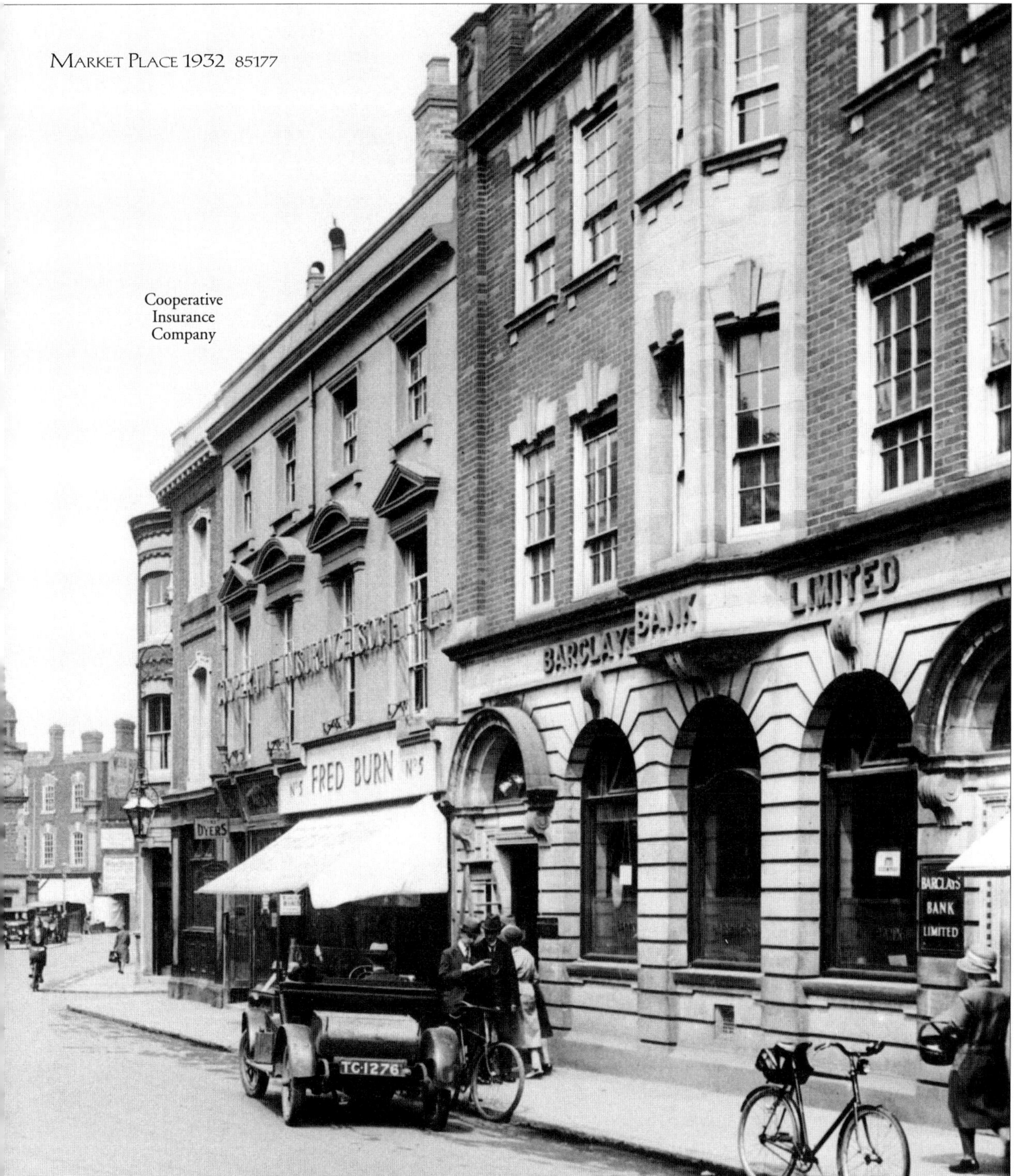

Market Place and the Town Centre

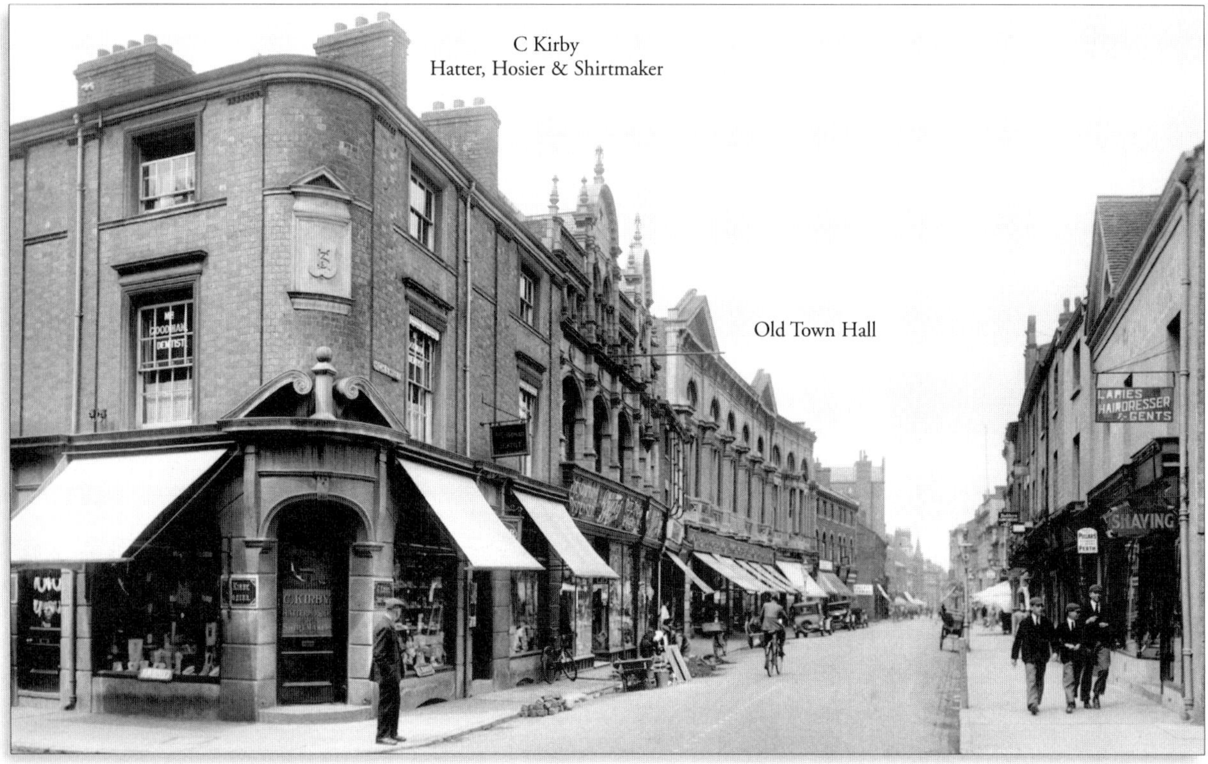

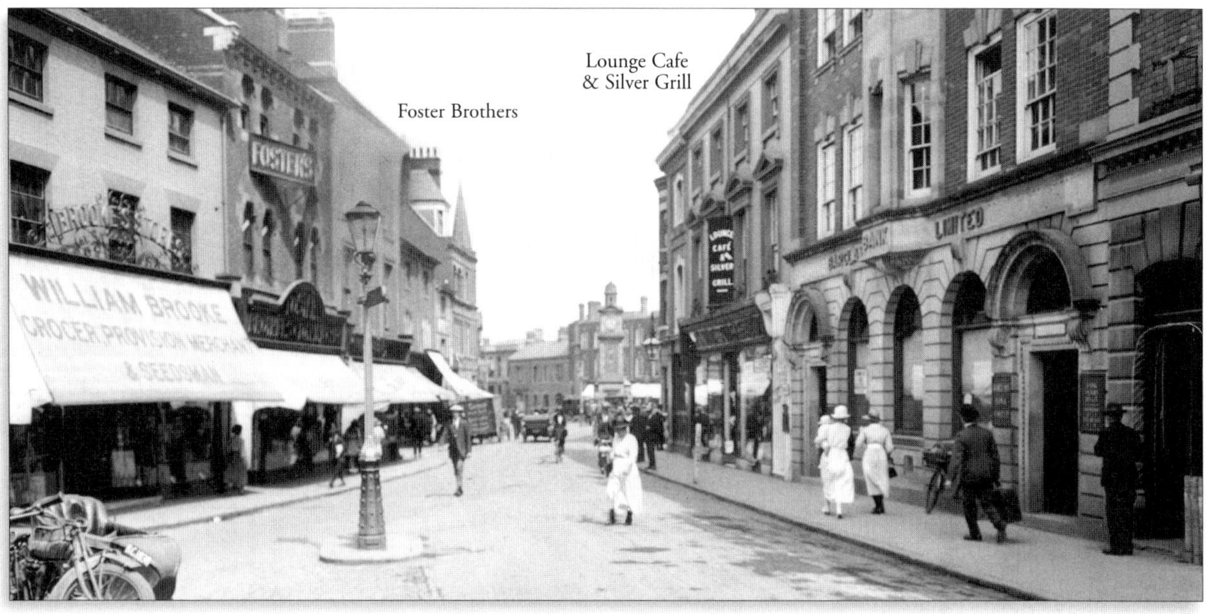

Above: The Junction of High Street 1922 72119

MARKET PLACE AND THE TOWN CENTRE

Left: HIGH STREET 1932 85178

The Town Hall, with its imitation Palladian style façade, was built on the site of the old Elborow School and Almshouses endowed by Richard Elborow in the 17th century. In 1900 the civic facility was moved to the Benn Buildings on the other side of the High Street (now Marks & Spencer); Rugby's first cinema (Leon Vint's Picture Palace) opened on the old site with an enlarged and extended first floor. Later known as the Rugby Palace Cinema, it was further extended in 1919. Damaged by fire in 1921, the site was taken over by Woolworth's, who replaced it in the 1950s with an ugly, featureless slab. Only the 1919 extension survives.

Below: HIGH STREET 1922 72124

Shopping was far less stressful in 1922 than it is today. There was little traffic, relatively few people and no yellow lines on the road. In the shop itself, the customer might well have been offered a chair while attentive staff fetched prospective purchases to be viewed. Packages would then be carried out to the customer's waiting car or trap, or perhaps a van or a delivery boy on a bicycle would deliver to their door. High staffing numbers were required to maintain this level of service, and a thriving retail trade provided alternative employment for many who might otherwise have gone into domestic service. The fortunes of Rugby School went hand in hand with that of the town. More boys meant a greater consumption of food, beer and fuel, and a greater need for services, such as washing and haircutting. Notice the display of goods outside Spencer's ironmongery. Ironmongers and even blacksmiths were commonplace.

One sad but very common sight after the Great War would have been the bands of unemployed ex-servicemen, often disabled, busking or simply begging in the streets.

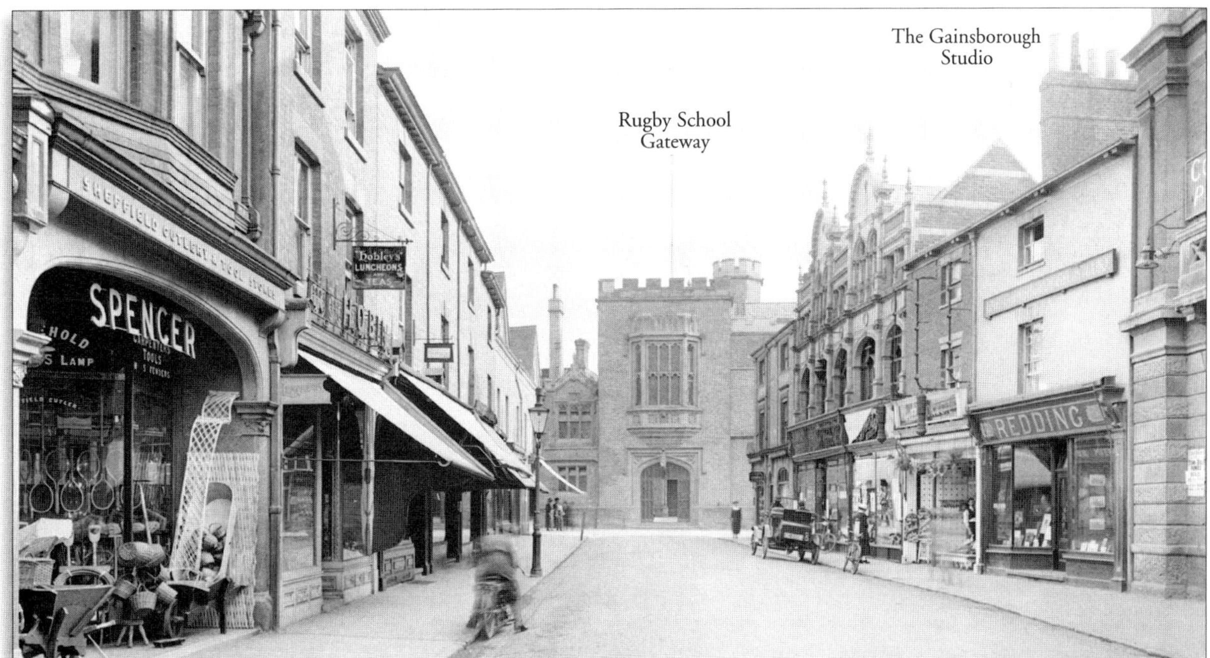

MARKET PLACE AND THE TOWN CENTRE

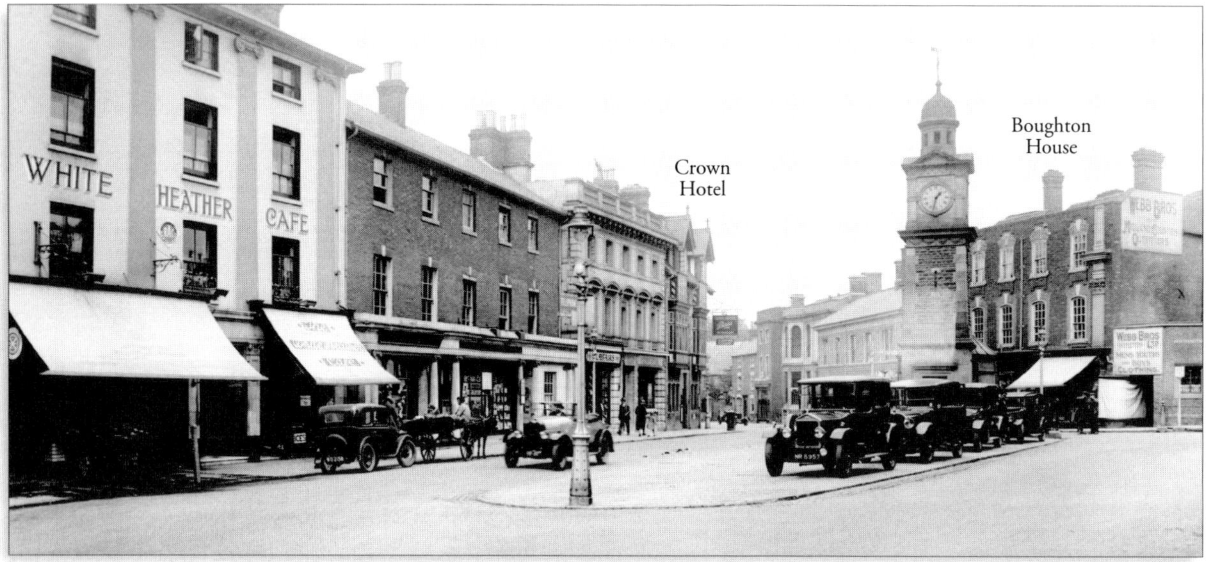

MARKET PLACE 1932 85180

The White Heather Café was originally the 18th-century Spread Eagle Hotel, later known as the Eagle Commercial Hotel. In 1868 it was sold to the Wesleyan Methodists, becoming a temperance hotel. The original façade can still be seen on the upper storey of the Lloyd's TSB. Next to the Eagle Hotel is a bookshop (once Billington and Lawrence, then George Over) built on the site of the medieval half-timbered, thatched Bear and Ragged Staff Inn, which closed in 1801. In 1980 this site became the entrance to the new Rugby Shopping Centre. The original 18th-century brickwork can still be seen over this entrance, which also retains the fine 19th-century Ionic columns.

Freed of livestock, the Saturday market became a more congenial place; it was thriving and prosperous, despite competition from a new Monday market introduced in 1883. The Market Place would have presented a colourful, bustling scene, loud with the cries of the market-traders, the rumble of cartwheels over cobbles, the barking of dogs and the shouts and laughter of children chasing through the crowded streets. There might well have been an Italian street-piano player to entertain the crowds, a monkey or bright-plumaged parrot perched upon his shoulder. Country people would have brought their goods into town by cart, perhaps hiring a carrier if they had no cart of their own. Some, perhaps, used a handcart, or even a backpack.

Much of the Market Place, Sheep Street and High Street had been cobbled since the 18th century, but the roads themselves were little more than dirt tracks, deeply rutted by cartwheels and extremely muddy in wet weather. Road improvements had begun as early as 1838, and by 1901 all of Rugby's main roads had been macadamised.

The Monday and Saturday markets continued to operate in Market Place until 1953, when they were moved, first to The Plaisance on Church Street, then to the Gas Street area opposite. Another trading day, Friday, was added, and Rugby's newest market — the popular Farmers' Market — was introduced in the year 2000, and in 2005 the Gas Street market returned to th High Street and Market Square area. Market Place,

Market Place and the Town Centre

High Street and Sheep Street are now shopper-friendly, pedestrianised areas with trees and raised flowerbeds, reproduction Victorian lampposts, bench seating and wrought iron bus shelters.

In 1900 the Town Hall moved to the Benn Building, which was erected on the opposite side of the High Street on the site of the old Shoulder of Mutton Inn, demolished in 1898. When the civic facilities moved to Newbold Road in 1936, Marks & Spencer took over the site, but its original elegant façade can still be seen. In 1961 the Town Hall moved yet again, this time to the Lawn Estate on Evreux Way.

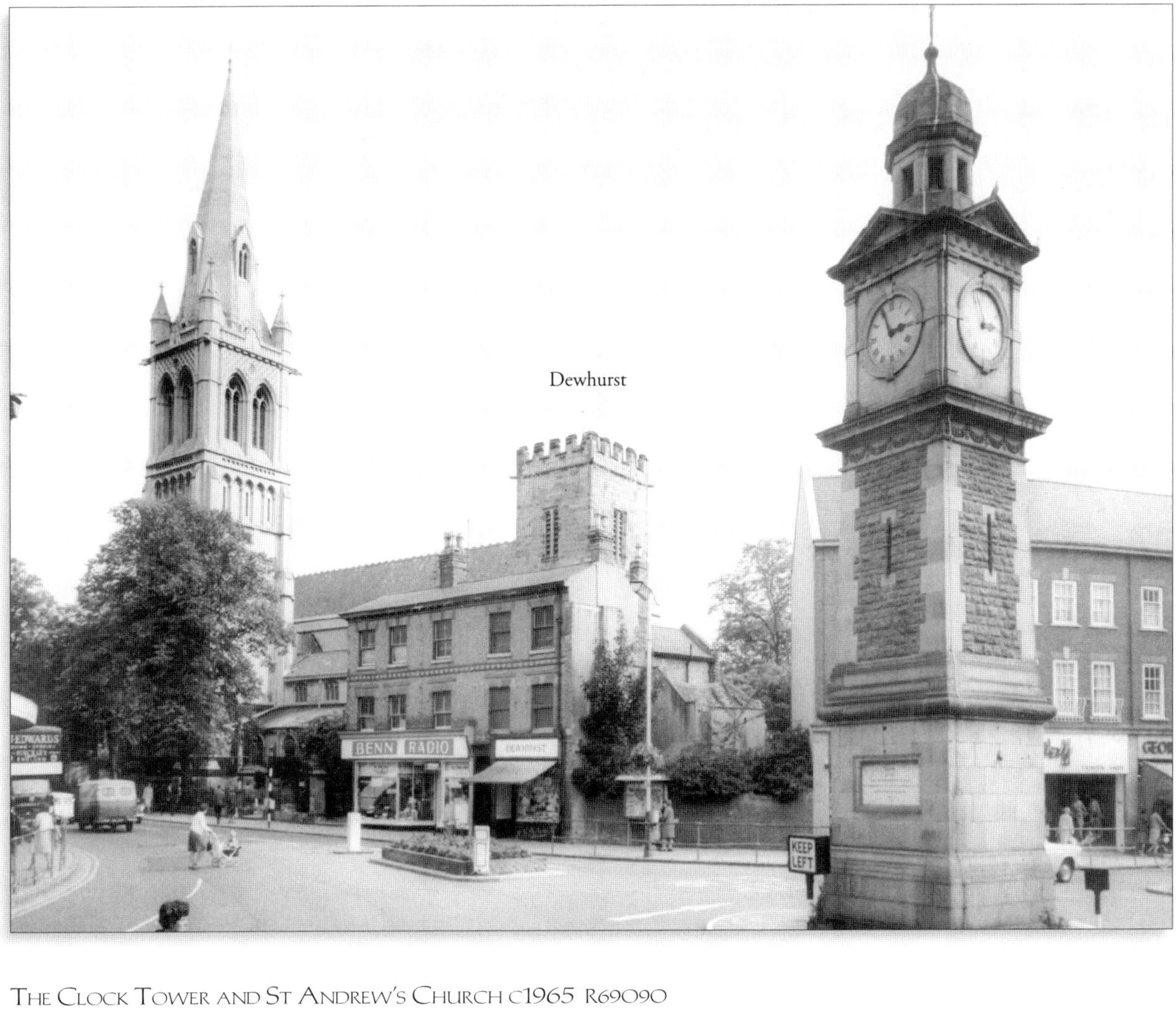

THE CLOCK TOWER AND ST ANDREW'S CHURCH c1965 R69090

By 1965 the George Hotel had disappeared, to be replaced by this uninteresting row of shops. Many small, independent shops have given way to chains such as Dewhurst the butchers, Burtons and Boots the chemist. Benn Radio has replaced the Grand Clothing Hall, remnant of a once great cloth industry. In 1932 the Clock Tower stood on a large paved area used for parking, but here it has been marooned on a small roundabout. By the 1990s it had become part of a pedestrianised shopping area.

Market Place and the Town Centre

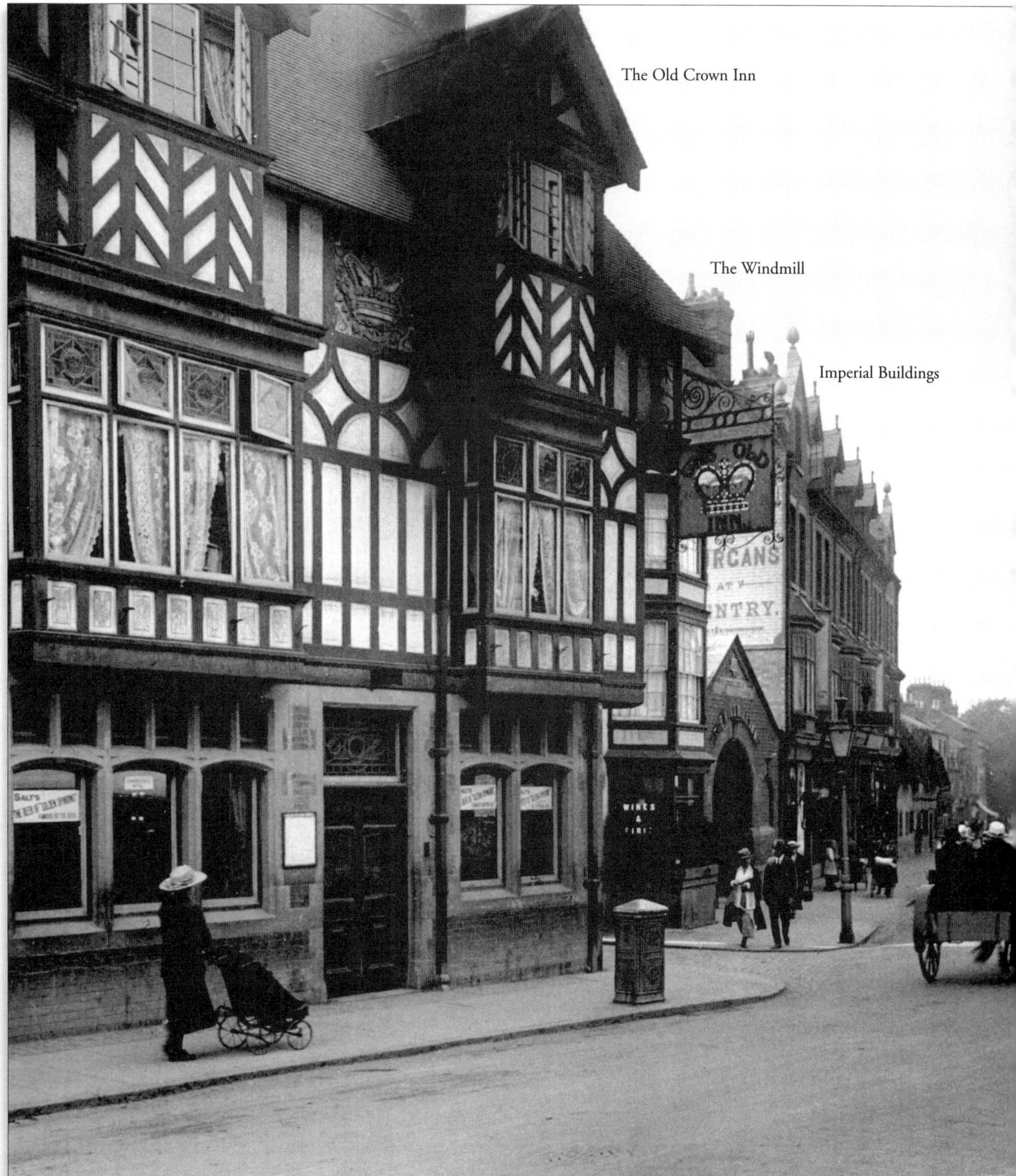

MARKET PLACE AND THE TOWN CENTRE

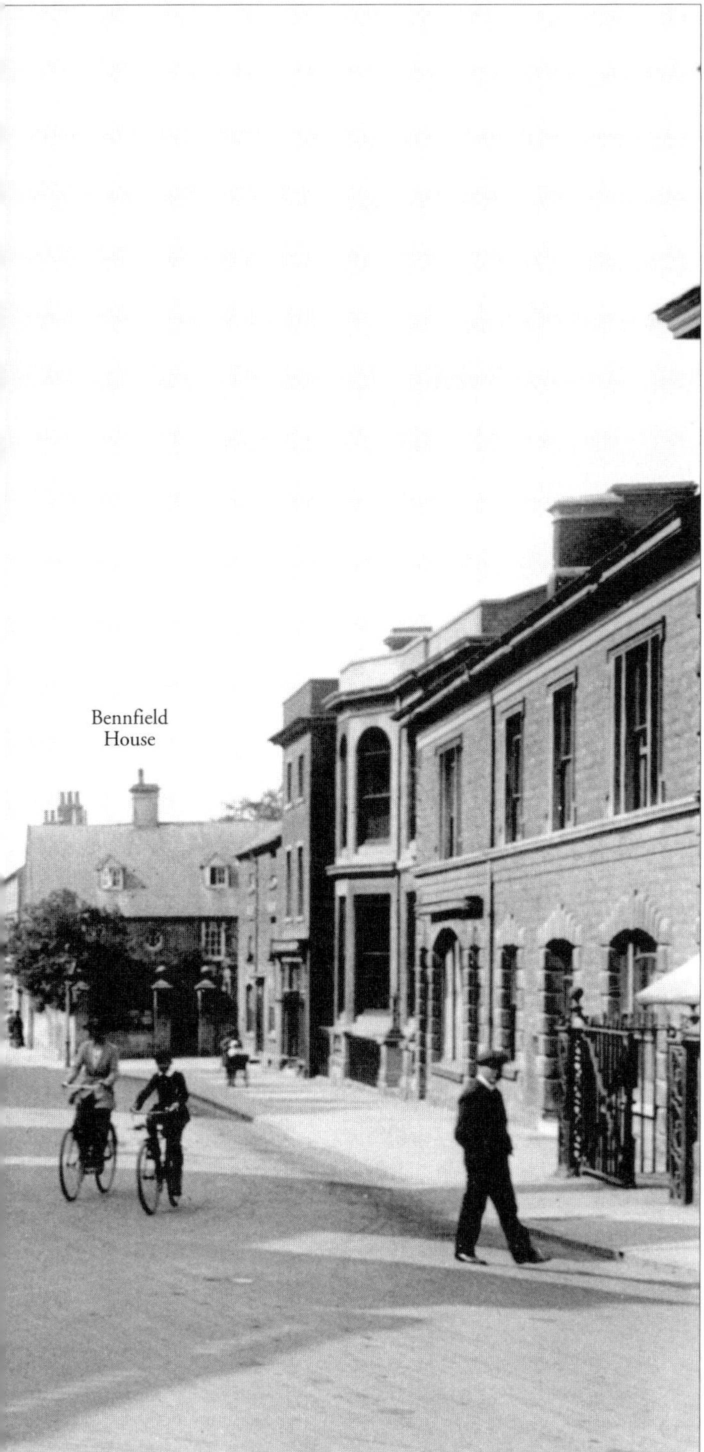

The Victorians loved to celebrate important occasions, and Queen Victoria's Golden Jubilee in June 1887 was celebrated with especial enthusiasm all over the country. Rugby commemorated the event with the Jubilee Clock Tower in Market Place, on the site of the old market cross (R69090, page 59). Designed by Mr Goodacre of Leicester, the Clock Tower was built by Parnell & Son at a cost of £530, which was raised by public subscription. It was formally handed over to the town in January 1889.

The Clock Tower's commemorative plaque was for many years obscured by the cabmen's shelter, which was erected about 1893. When the shelter was taken down in 1933, the existence of the plaque came as a surprise to many younger Rugbeians. The inscription reads: 'Erected by the Town and Neighbourhood of Rugby To commemorate the fiftieth Anniversary of Queen Victoria's Accession. 1887'.

NORTH STREET 1922 72127

The Crown was built in 1887 on the site of a late 17th-century house that later became the original Old Crown Inn, a name still apparent on the inn sign seen here. The 18th-century Windmill Inn beyond (originally Windmill House) was named for its curiously tall, narrow shape. First recorded as an inn in 1809, it is now the Rugby Tavern. Dogge Lane, which ran between the two inns, became Windmill Lane in the 1850s, and the Imperial Buildings, seen to the right of the Windmill, were erected in 1837.

Market Place and the Town Centre

The Clock Tower is 43 feet 6 inches high; it is built of Darley Dale stone, partly filled with Northampton iron-stone, on a base of grey Aberdeen granite. Until the early years of the 20th century, there was an underground gentlemen's convenience at its foot. The four-dialled clock, which had to be rewound each week, was made by Evans & Sons, Soho Clock Factory, Birmingham, and was originally lit by four gas jets on each face. Electricity now both runs the clock and illuminates the faces.

In 1894, many of the 17th-century buildings between Market Place and Chapel Street were pulled down, leaving a small 15th-century house on the corner of Chapel Street and Drury Lane, just off Sheep Street. Apart from the west tower of St Andrew's, this is Rugby's oldest building, although only the cob end wall is truly original. It is believed to be the butcher's shop, Tew's, referred to in Thomas Hughes's 'Tom Brown's Schooldays', where Tom bought a steak for a black eye.

In the past seventy years, few streets in Rugby have changed quite as much as North Street. Apart from the Crown Inn and the Windmill Inn (now the Rugby Tavern), none of the buildings seen in this street in 1922 (opposite) still remain. The thatched cottages were demolished in 1933, when Rugby Portland Cement acquired the site for their Crown House offices. These later moved to Crown House (renamed RMC House) at the corner of Corporation Street and Evreux Way. The NatWest Bank now occupies the old Crown House site.

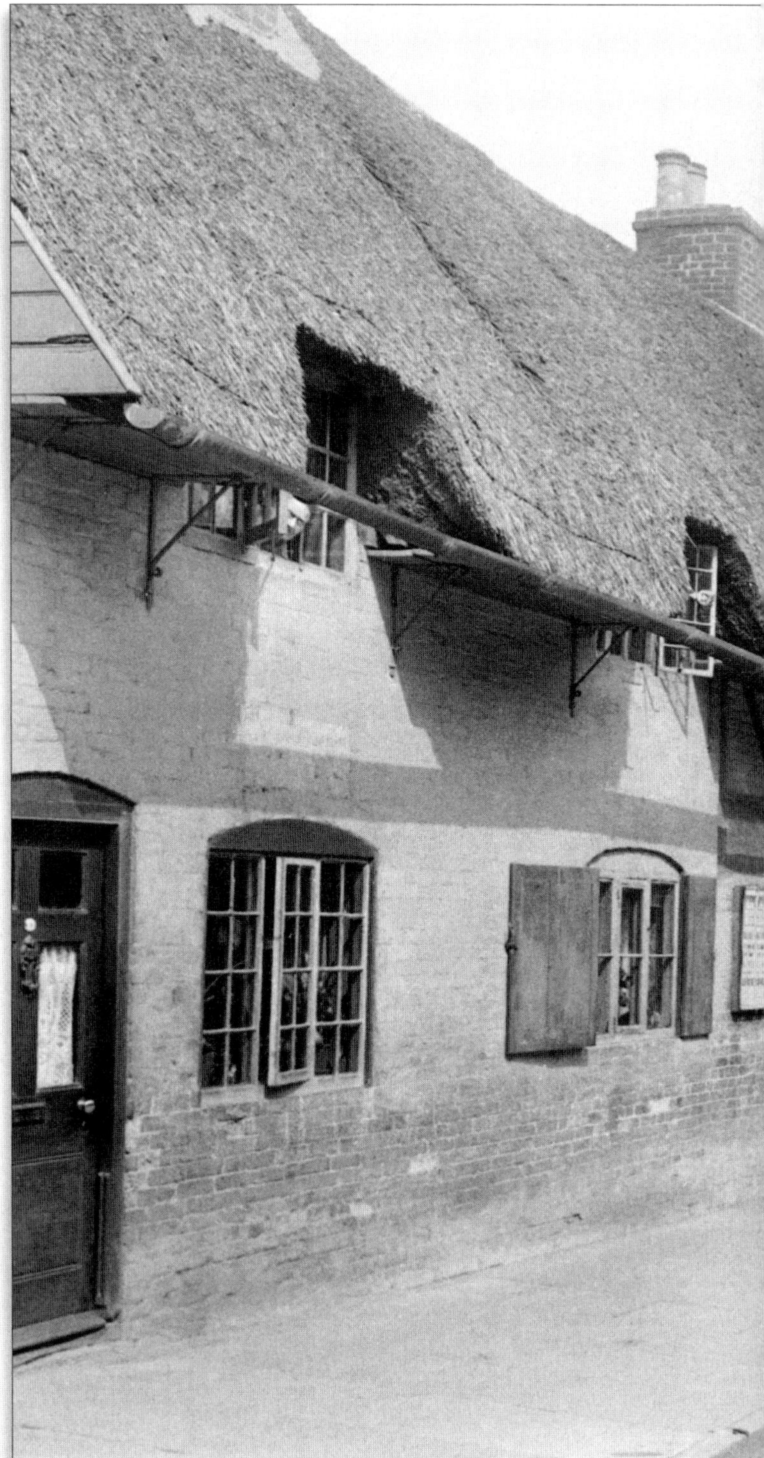

OLD HOUSES, NORTH STREET 1922 72120

Dating from the end of the reign of Elizabeth I, these thatched cottages originally had timber frames filled with lath and plaster. In the early 18th century this was replaced with brick noggin. Later, the two cottages on the far left were completely rebuilt in brick. They were demolished in 1933.

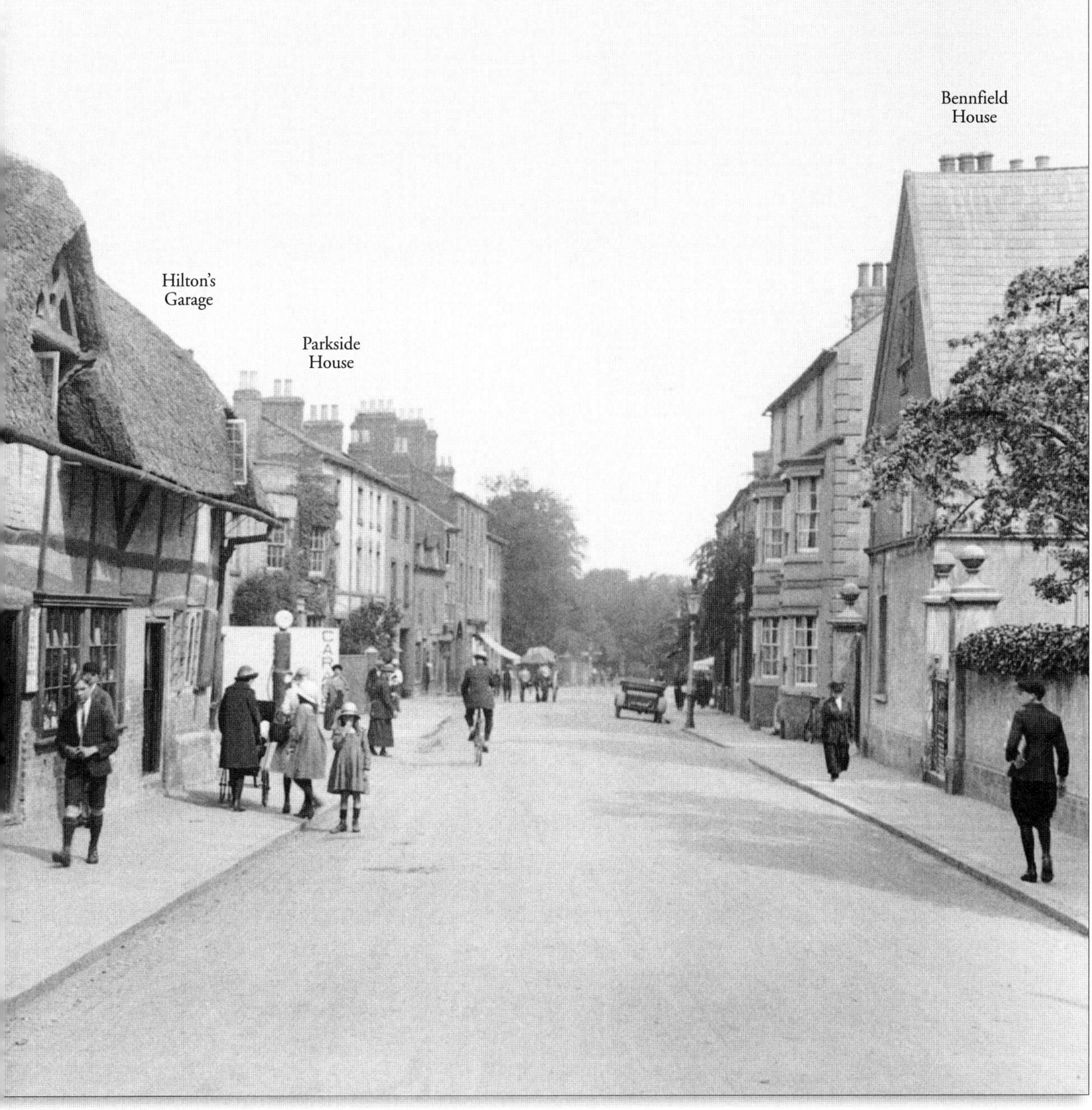

Market Place and the Town Centre

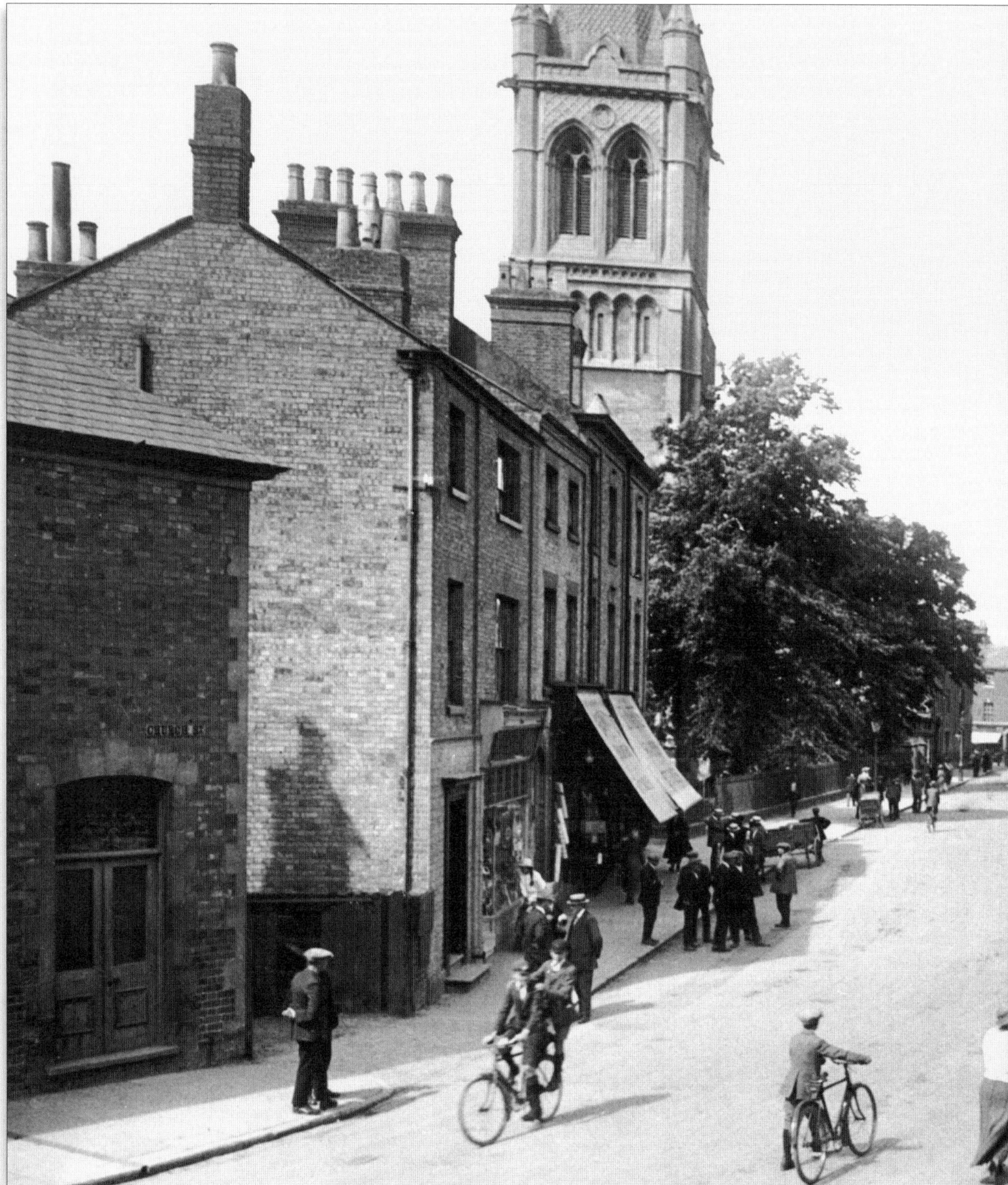

CHURCH STREET 1922 72117

East from the Clock Tower runs Church Street, stretching from St Andrew's Church to Clifton Road. The buildings on the left and on the far right still survive, but the building to the right of Lloyd's Bank has been replaced by a modern, uninspired HSBC (formerly Midland Bank) building. The lamp-post in the centre of the street has now disappeared, and the road in the forefront of the picture is now divided by a long, raised, flower-filled central reservation.

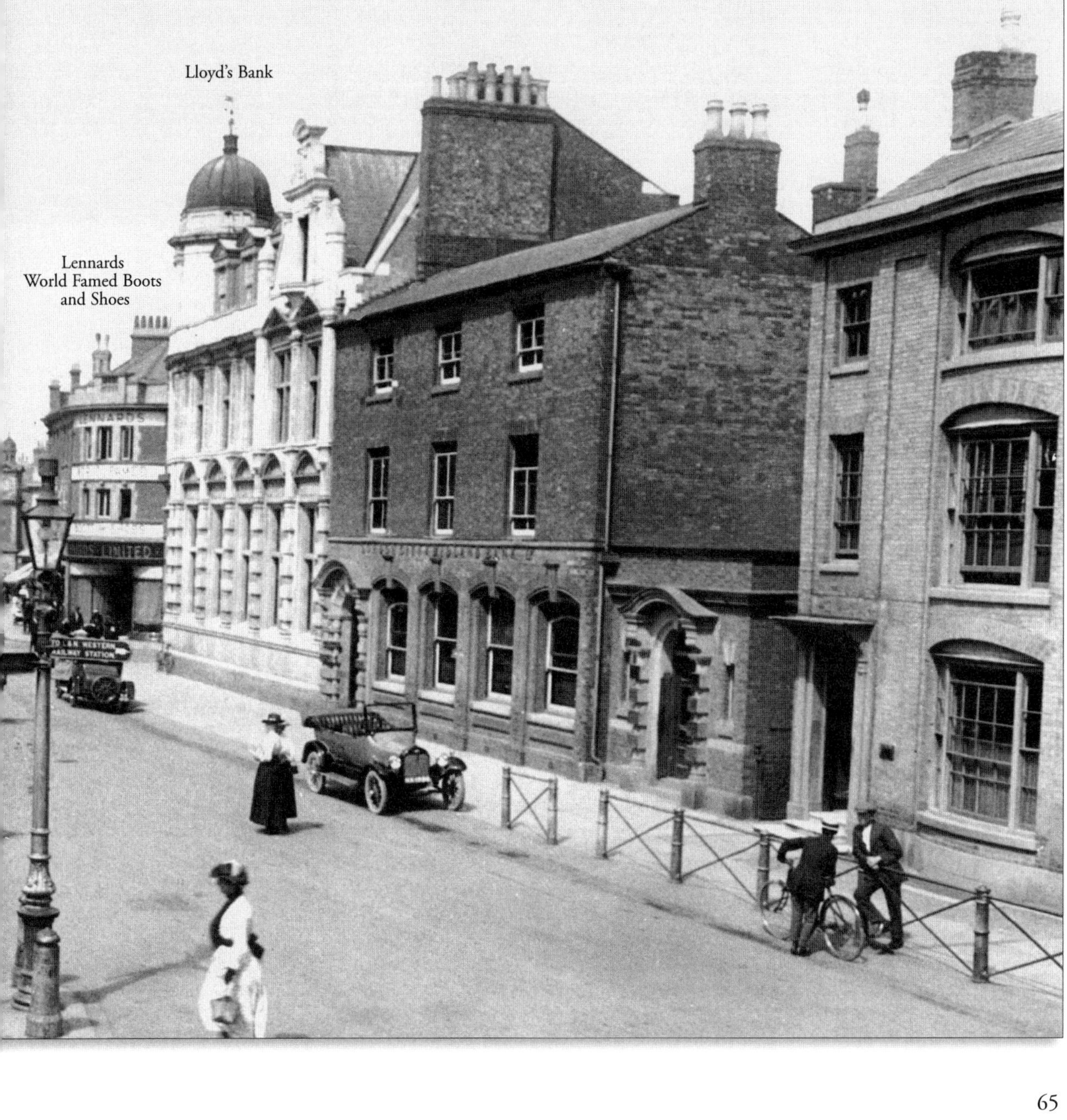

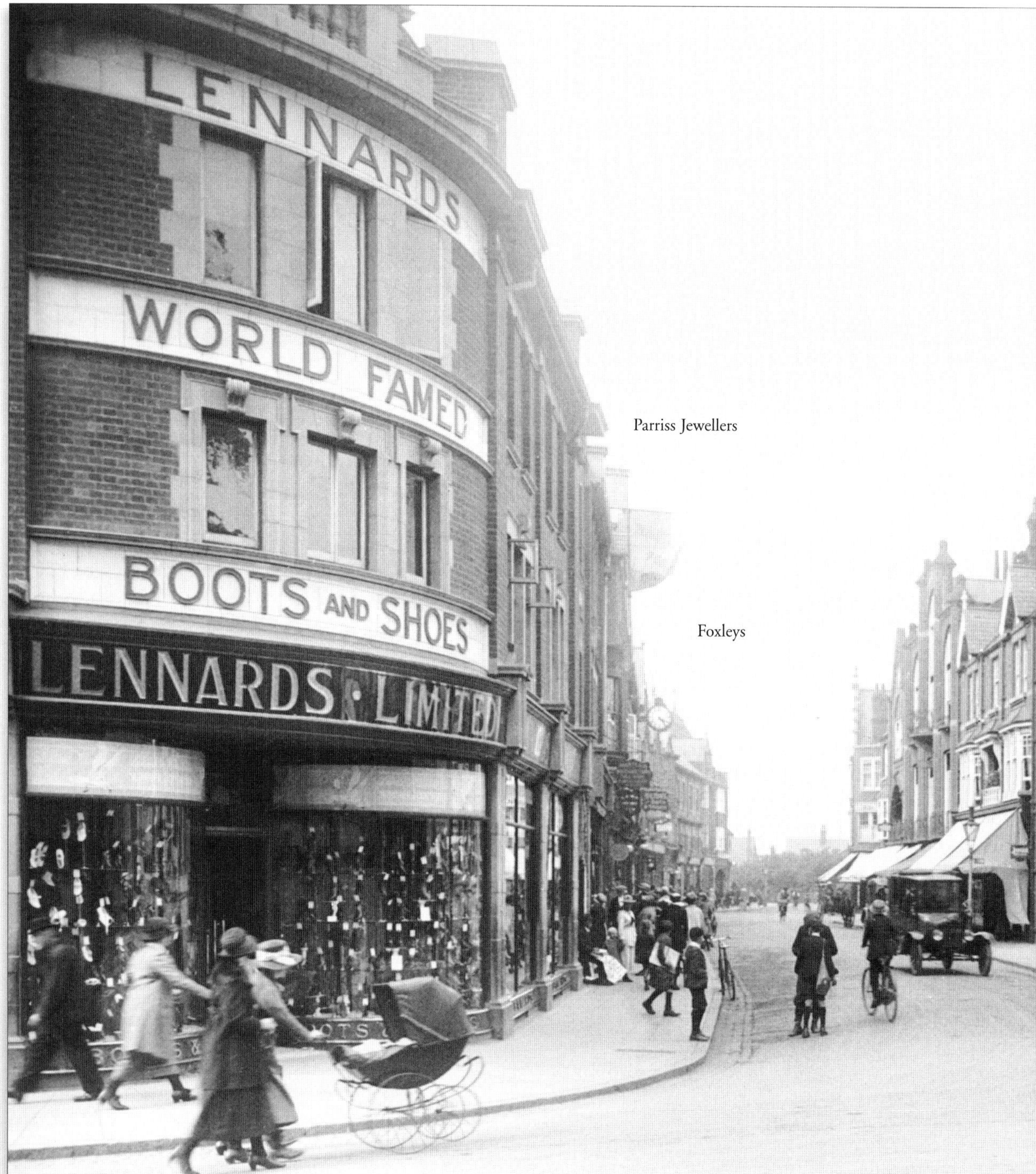

Parriss Jewellers

Foxleys

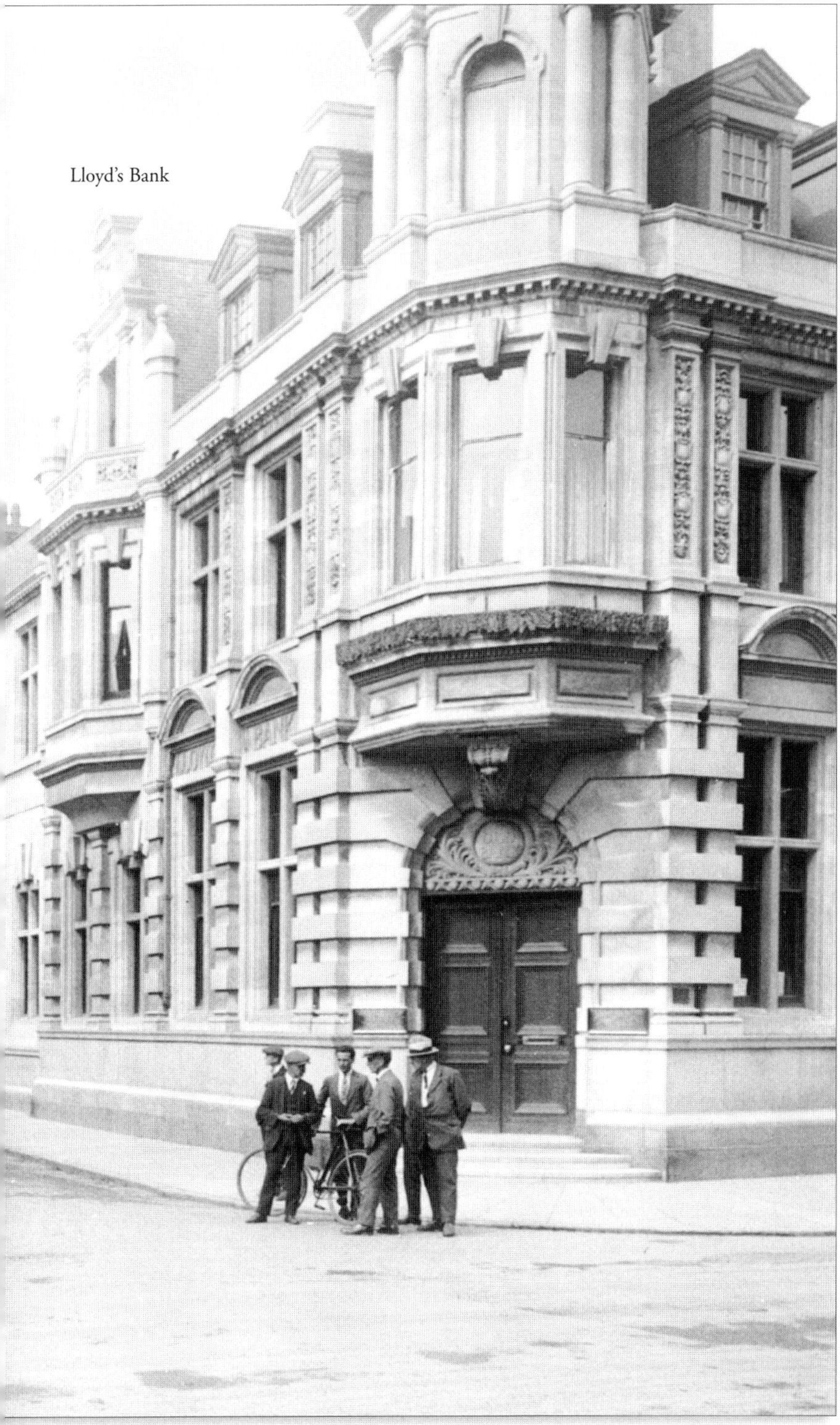

Lloyd's Bank

REGENT STREET 1922 72128

When Regent Street was created in 1902, Moat House — a large Regency building with arched Gothic doorways — was demolished to make way for the new street and for the Lloyd's Bank (right), built in 1906. Lennards, built in 1915, was still trading in Rugby until the late 1980s, when it became Tandem Shoes. Today, it is an estate agency, but the Lennards name can still clearly be seen in the brickwork. A later two-storey bank extension now hides the end wall with the large advertising poster seen at the centre of this picture. The poster was an advert for the shop below, Adnitts, which is now a café bar.

Market Place and the Town Centre

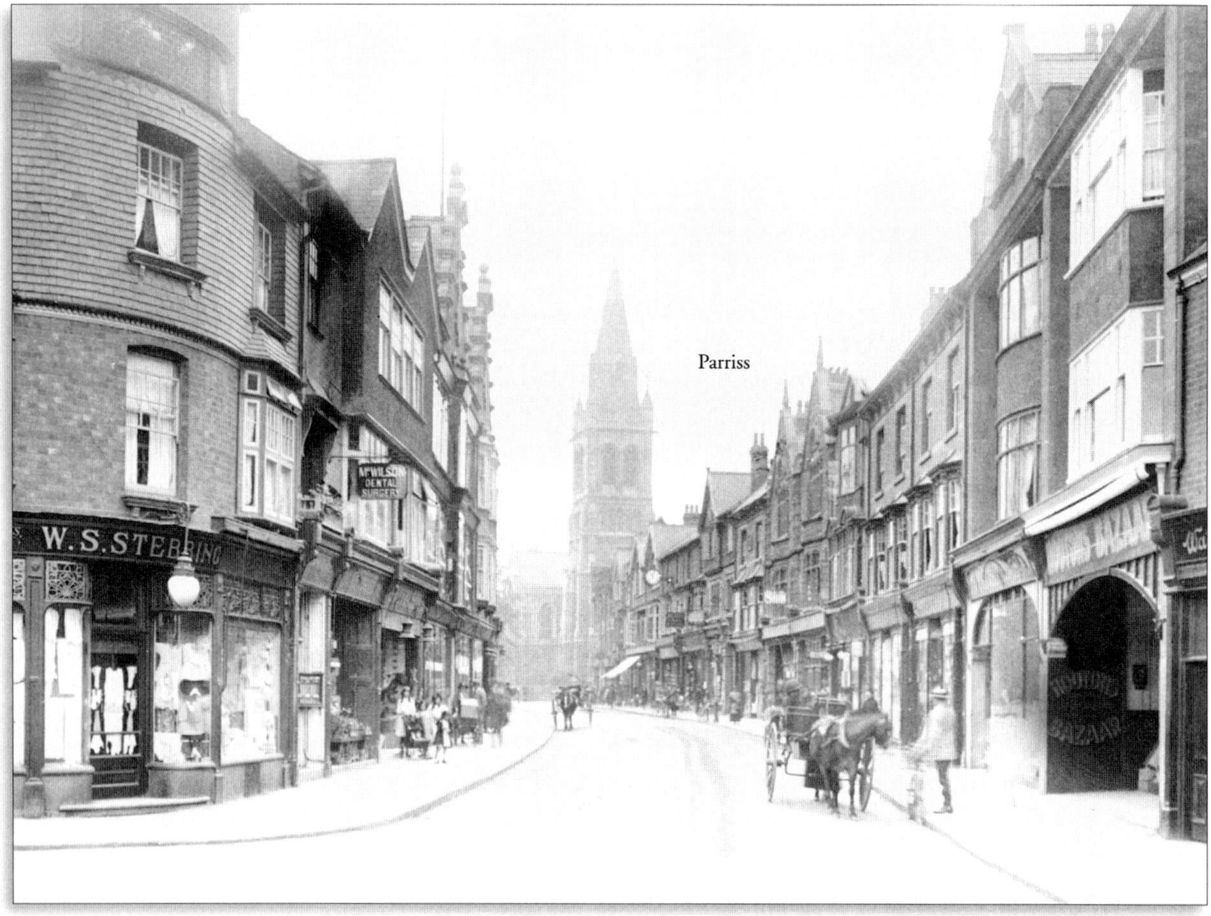

Regent Street 1922 72129

Seen here from Regent Place, Regent Street is one of Rugby's least changed areas. Foxley's (far right) is on the same site today, as is Parriss the Jewellers with its clock above the shop. Regent Street once boasted Rugby's first and last internet café, now gone.

Bennfield House, built in 1669, stood in extensive grounds on the eastern side of North Street (72120, page 63). The 17th-century brick pillars and finials at its gates were repeated at the entrance to some open ground, known as Bennfield, on the western side of the street. The double-fronted house next to Bennfield House was built on Bennfield House land in the 18th century. Bennfield House was demolished in 1930 to make way for the North Street Post Office (now replaced by Barclay's Bank). Hilton's Garage was built on the Bennfield in 1922.

Parkside House, a double bow-fronted Regency building, was demolished in 1930, the site being taken over by Hilton's Garage; it disappeared in 1978 to make way for a service entrance to the new Rugby Shopping Centre.

By the mid 19th century, the increase in the number of factories, combined with a fast and efficient transport system, led to vastly increased competition in the market place, with local craftsmen facing increased competition from mass-produced factory goods. This led to a consumer revolution in which advertising became of paramount importance. On every available wall, advertisements for brands such as Pear's Soap and Robin Starch appeared, displayed on colourful — and now very collectable — enamel signs. Shops strove to increase their visibility with ornate, wrought iron signs, large painted advertisements or with names fashioned in stone or brickwork. Banks, in particular, vied to outdo each other in ostentation in order to impress and attract customers.

Window dressing became a subject of particular interest amongst shopkeepers. The Rugby Advertiser of June 1910, in its account of the Rugby Shopping Festival, notes that in the things-to-wear class of the window-dressing competition, Messrs Adnitts won first prize with a seascape of 'white embroideries and embroidered muslins' and 'a model of a brig, in full sail, made of cardboard and covered with embroideries'.

Even as early as 1910, the threat to small business from larger chains was clear even to the general public. In her winning entry for the Shopping Festival's 'Why I Shop in Rugby' essay competition, Mrs Norton of Albert Street states that she shops in Rugby: ' … firstly, because it is more convenient; secondly, because it is more economical; thirdly, because it is more pleasant; and fourthly, because it is my duty ... Now and again we hear it prophesied that in the time to come there will be no private shops, for they will all have been swallowed up by the big stores. May that day be far distant!'

Rugby, like most small towns today, sees new shops come and go — sometimes within months. The same large chains now dominate most town and city centres, a process seen in the presence of shops such as Dewhursts Butchers and Burtons in Rugby by 1932, although it had started much earlier. The greater buying power of these chains enabled a competitive pricing that eventually forced many small, independent businesses out of the market. Salters of Rugby, a long-established outfitter in the High Street, is one of the few to have survived.

Without refrigerators or freezers, the housewife of the 19th and earlier 20th century had to shop daily, either carrying her shopping home in a basket or having it delivered, perhaps by a boy on a bicycle — a situation best served by several small shops supplying different residential areas. Ironmongers' shops supplied brooms and tin baths and black lead for the stove; drapers' and haberdashers' shops supplied the fabric and trimmings for home-made clothes.

Today, things are very different. The shops in the town centre supply greetings cards, holidays, electrical goods and mobile phones. Drapers' shops, milliners, haberdashers and independent outfitters (with the exception of Salters) have given way to the large, ubiquitous clothing chains. The ironmongers, the grocers and the butchers have disappeared from the streets, their trade now carried out by huge out-of-town supermarkets. Some things, however, have remained the same: there are still plenty of cafés in which to meet friends or simply take a break from shopping, and there are still plenty of pubs and hairdressers.

In the past century, far too much of Rugby's historical and architectural heritage has been destroyed; but the town is beginning to recover. The grim and unwelcoming Rugby Shopping Centre was revamped in the 1990s as the Clock Towers, a much brighter and more inviting place altogether. The Market Place area, now closed to most traffic, is often enlivened by buskers and other street entertainers, and it is to be hoped that soon the decayed Chapel Street area will finally be redeveloped, attracting new business to the town.

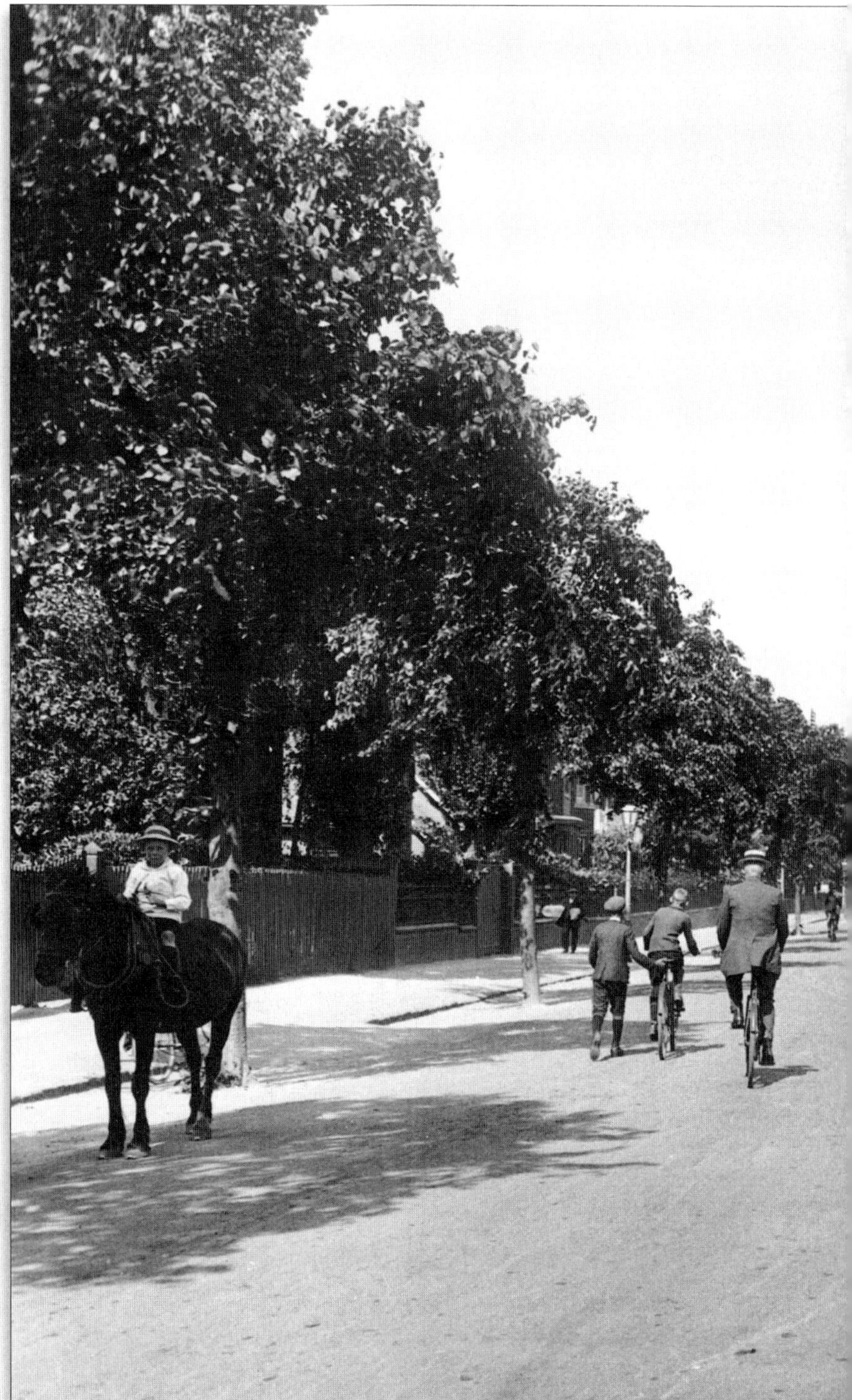

CLIFTON ROAD 1922 72121

In this charming view of Clifton Road everyone wears a hat, a strictly-observed fashion rule that persisted into the 1960s. By 1922 there were already quite a number of cars around, but foot power, carts and traps, horses and bicycles were still the only affordable forms of transport for many people. Notice the man with the handcart in the centre of the photograph. He might well be a railway porter, carrying luggage from the station. Behind the camera, Clifton Road runs down to Clifton (or Moreton) Brook. Once, this was the last stage of Rugby School's spring brook-jumping run, which began at Brownsover Mill. The area has been known as Butler's Leap since 1849, when 17-year-old Arthur Butler cleared the fence and brook in one bound.

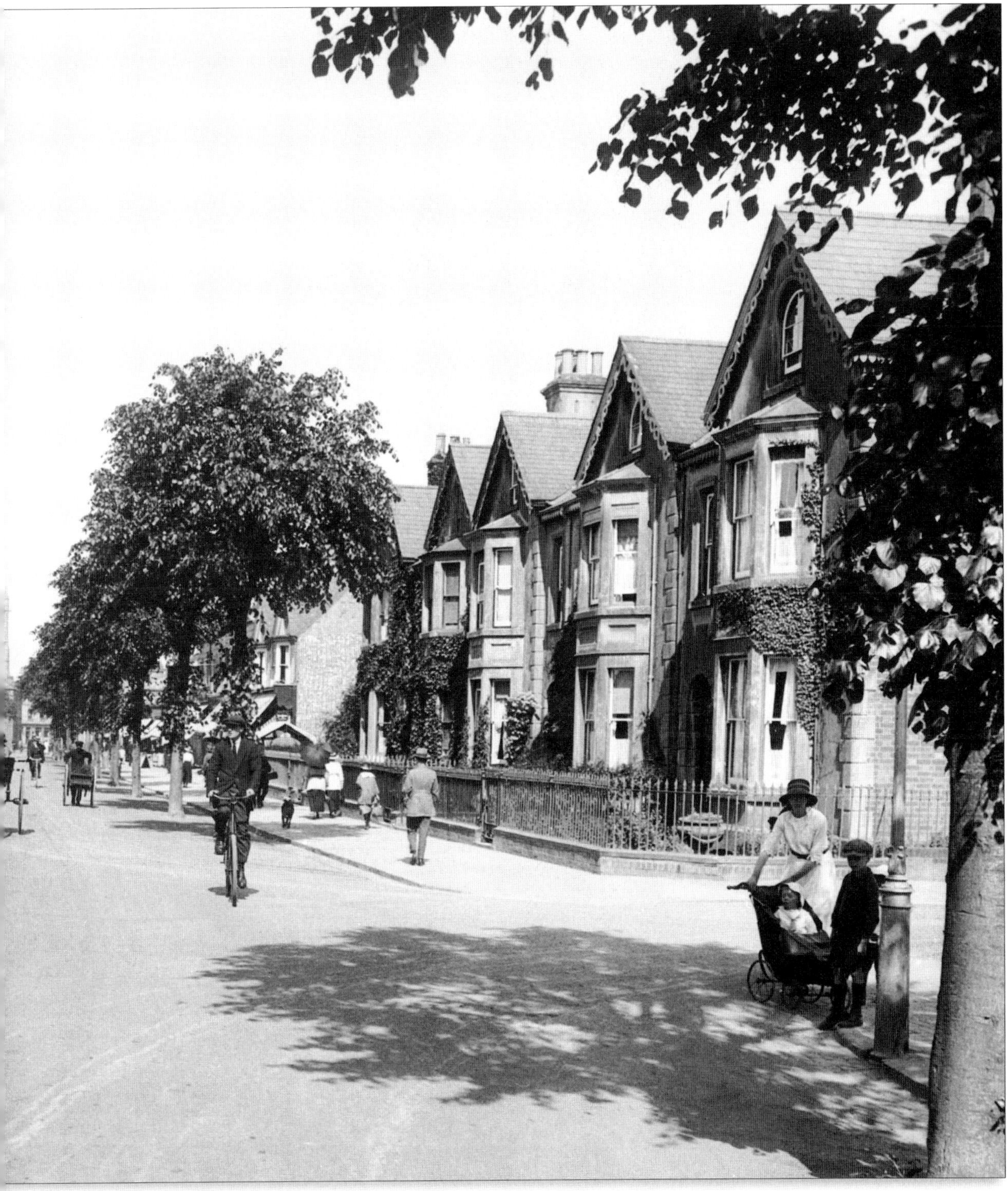

Ordnance Survey Map

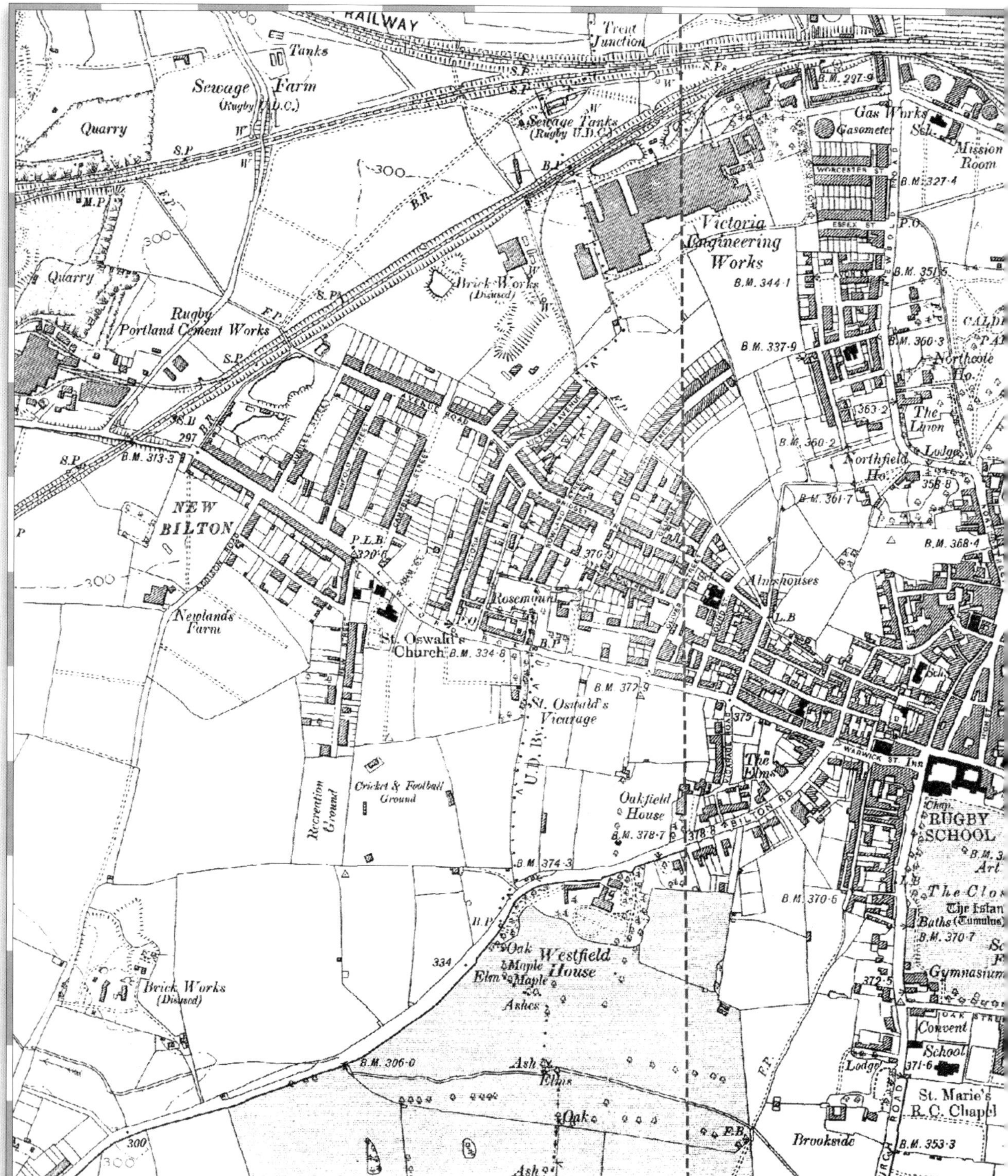

Ordnance Survey Map

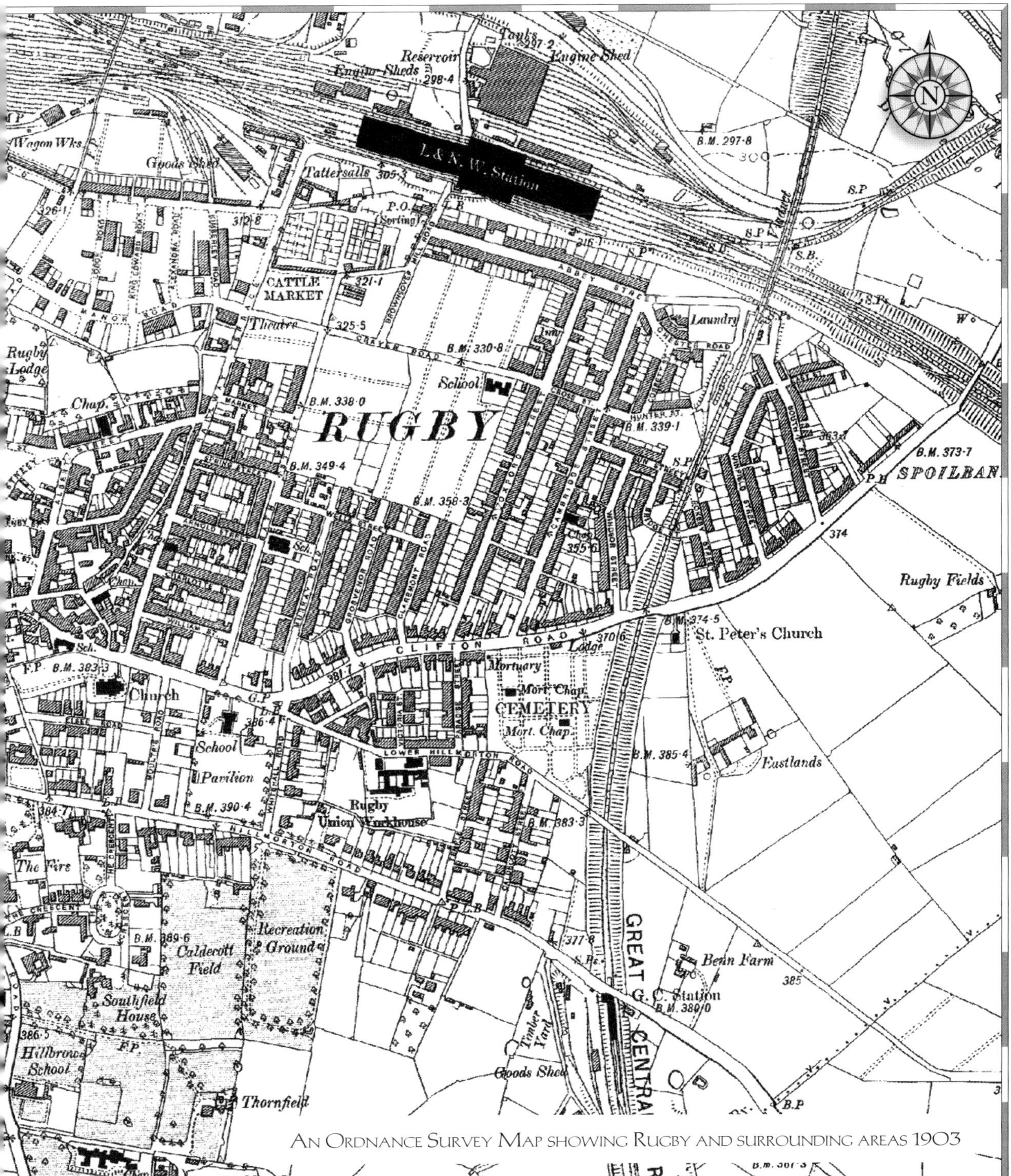

An Ordnance Survey Map showing Rugby and surrounding areas 1903

ROUND AND ABOUT

OPENED in 1904, Caldecott Park was designed by Mr Edward Thomas of Aughton, Lancashire, who won £20 for his plan (a triangular park with a large clump of trees in the centre) in a newspaper competition. The trees, originally part of the manorial ash grove, are now mainly oaks. His design also included 'three conveniences suitably clad' and a small lake in the centre of the park, which had to be filled in during the 1920s because of problems with leakage. It was replaced with an ornamental garden at a cost of £200.

For those in earlier days who worked long hours and raised their families in poor and often cramped accommodation, a stroll in Caldecott Park and Sunday concerts at the bandstand (overleaf) must have felt like a holiday. For the children, there were swings by the Park Road side gate, but they were chained and locked on Sundays — the Lord's Day. The playground has now been moved to the right of the main entrance, and Sunday use is, of course, no longer prohibited.

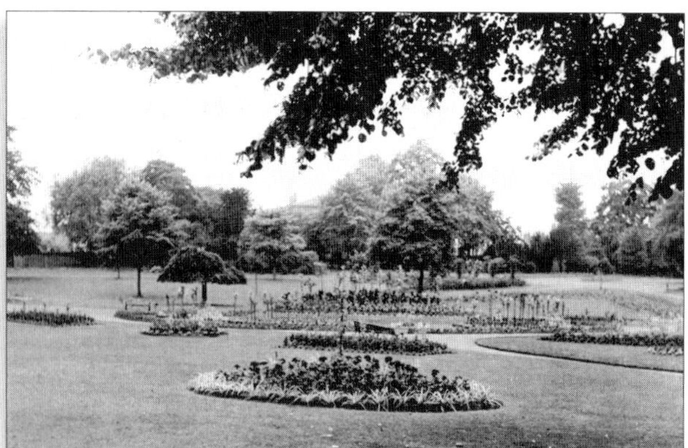

Caldecott Park c1960 R69043

Caldecott Park 1922 72138

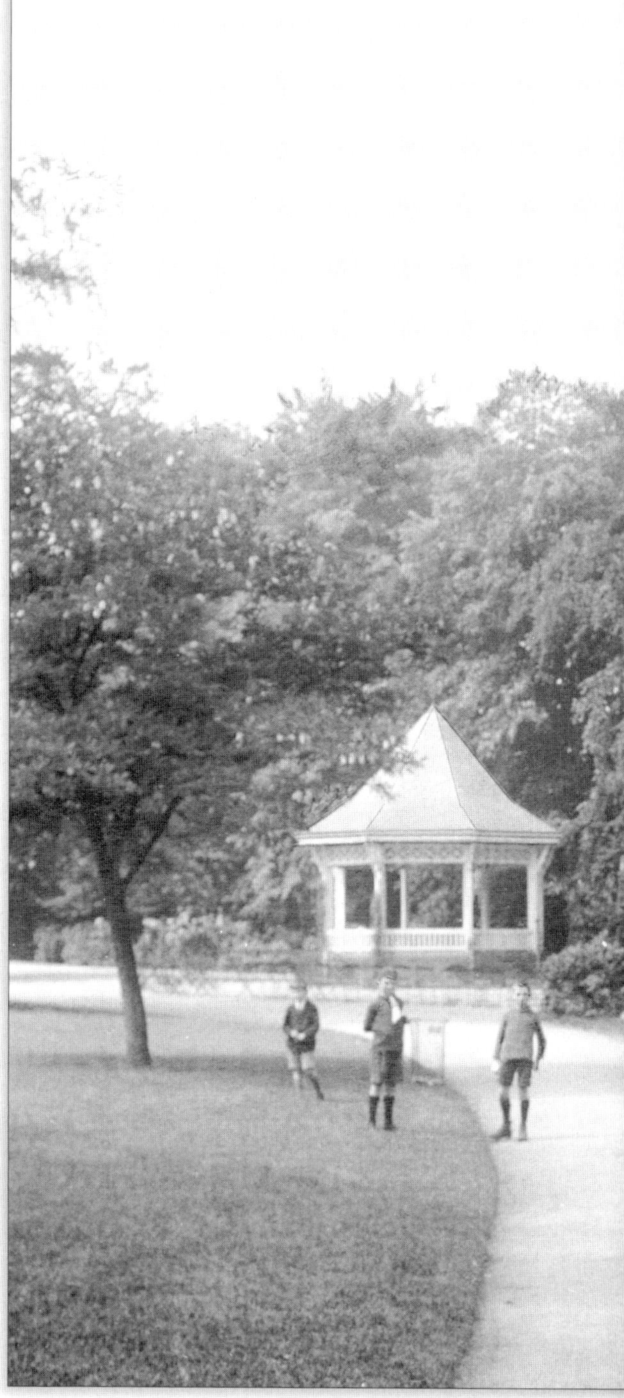

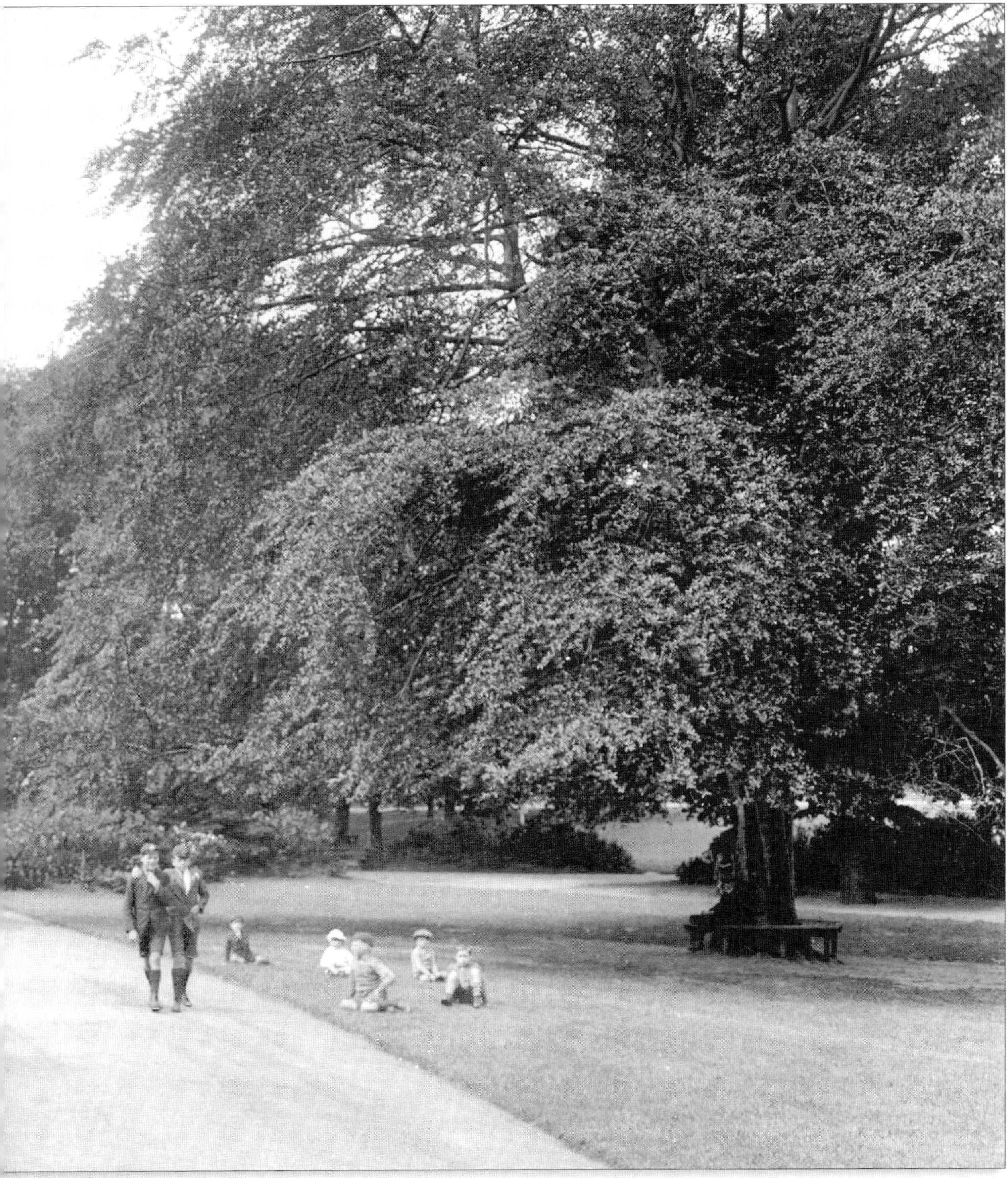

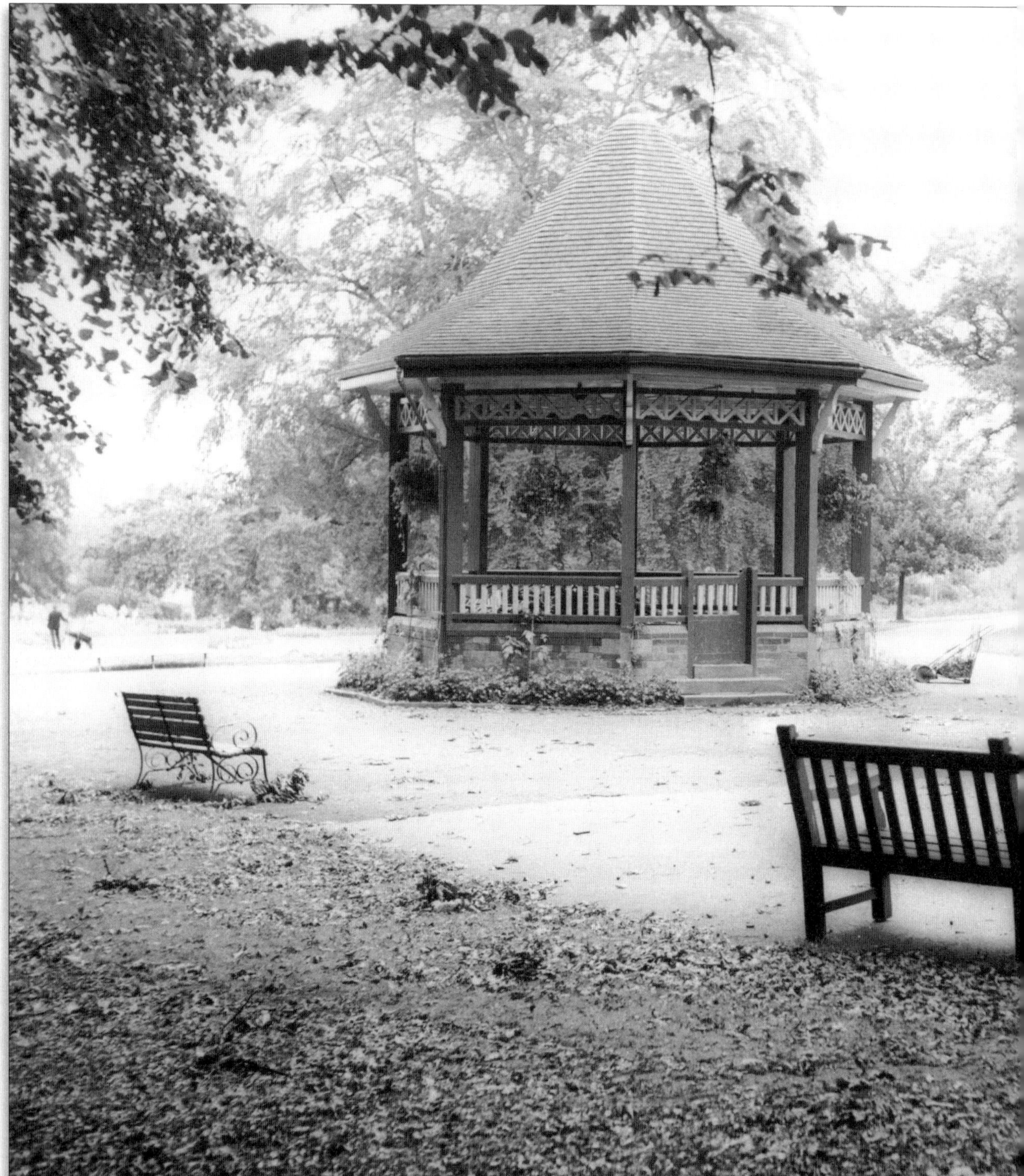

ROUND AND ABOUT

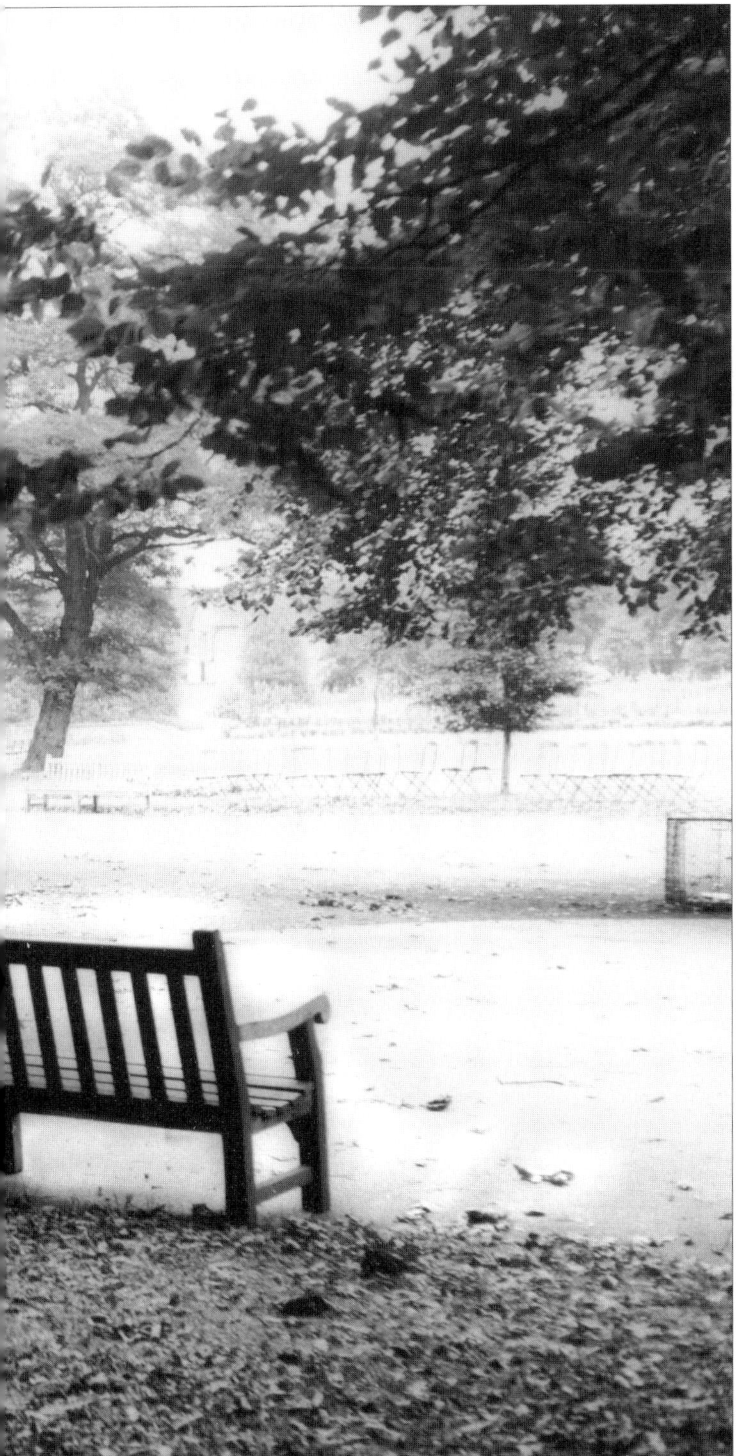

Over the years, the Parks Department has been responsible for many fine floral displays commemorating special events. A floral crown marked the Coronation of King George VI in 1937, and in 1953, to commemorate the Coronation of Queen Elizabeth II, a fragrant raised garden was created for the blind with a descriptive Braille plaque beside each aromatic plant. Other displays have included the Borough Coat of Arms and the Floral Steps. The tradition has continued, and in 1999 the Rugby World Cup was commemorated with a floral display featuring a rugby ball.

During the Second World War, when railway use was discouraged and seaside beaches were often designated as military zones, Rugby Council organised a 'Holidays at Home' scheme to entertain local people. A temporary concert stand was built in front of the bandstand in 1942, and over 80 attractions were held in the park during 1943, including concerts by both local and well-known bands and orchestras, with up to 1,000 people attending. The stand was removed in 1949, and when Rugby Town Hall was enlarged in 1979, the Coronation gates at the entrance to the Park were moved to their present position.

THE BANDSTAND C1965 R69085

This six-sided bandstand was erected by Fawcett's (local cabinet-makers and builders) in around 1910, when Sunday concerts were still very popular. It is no longer in use.

Another recreation ground available to Rugbeians was the Whitehall Recreation Ground on Hillmorton Road, which housed a 28-ton, armoured First World War tank presented to the town in 1919, in recognition of contributions to National War Savings. In 1940 the tank was sold for scrap as part of a new war effort.

Queen Victoria's Golden Jubilee was celebrated not only with the Clock Tower, but also with an extensive tree-planting project along selected roads leading into Rugby (see Clifton Road overleaf).

Dunchurch, 4 miles to the south-west of Rugby, is a small village of thatched cottages and popular public houses and restaurants. The village green boasts a two-seater set of stocks (last used in 1866) and a thatched bus shelter. At the cross-roads stands the market cross on a stepped, medieval base, the cross itself replaced in 1813 by a milestone.

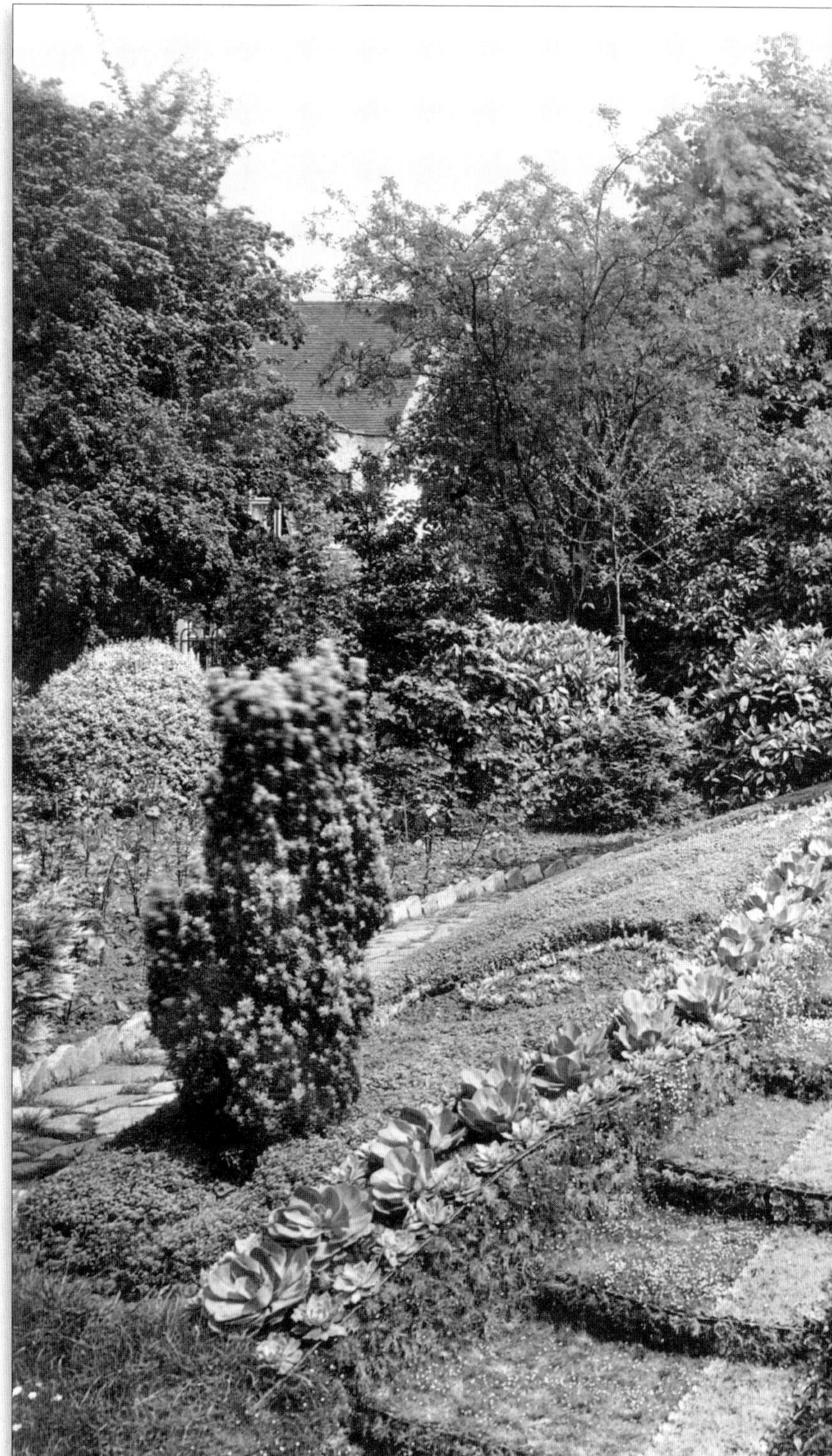

The Floral Steps 1932 85193

At the top of this popular display stood the statue 'Echo', donated by the Rugby solicitor H W Worthington. When he died in 1943, his ashes were scattered in the park. The statue became affectionately known as 'Peter Pan'.

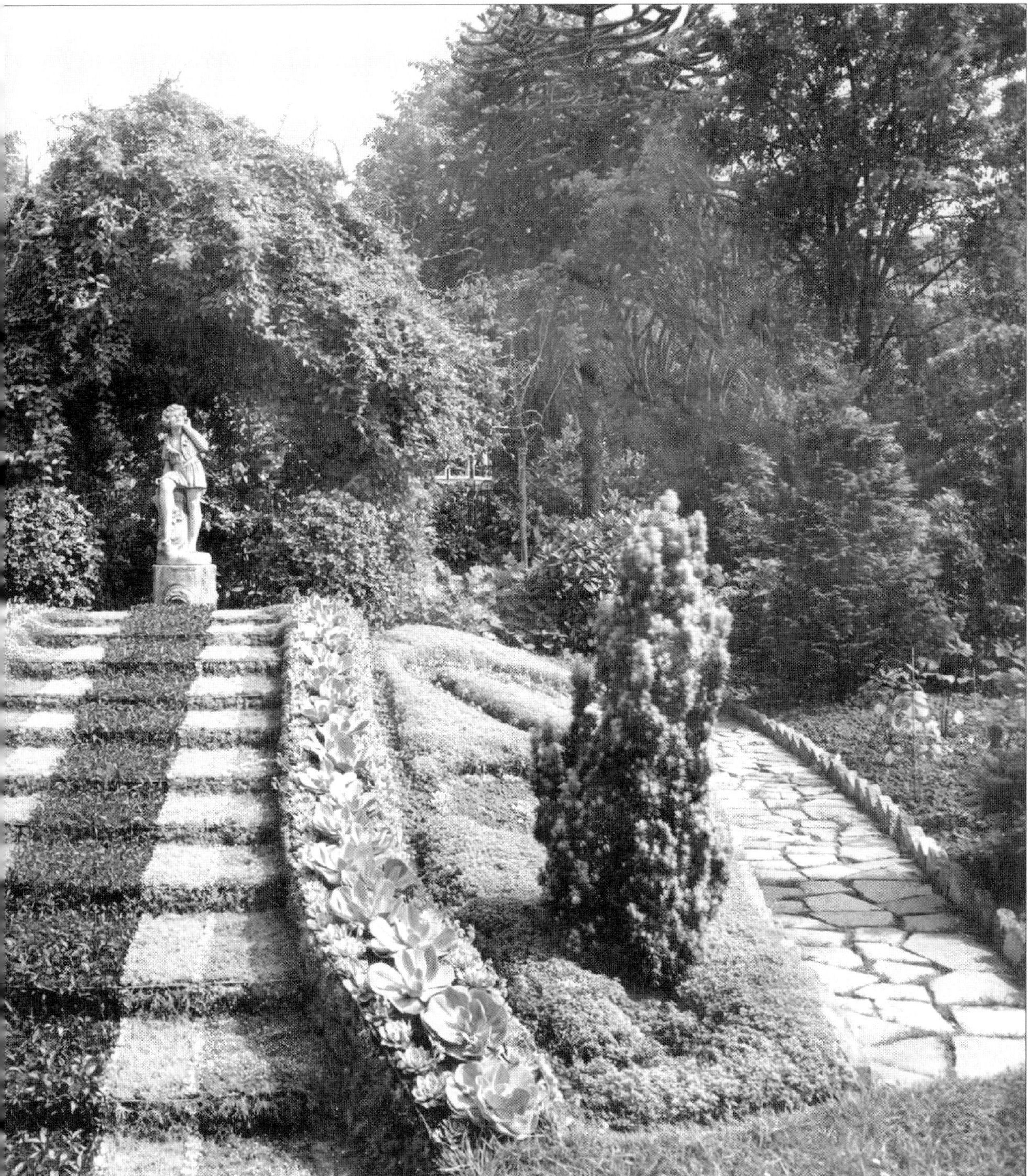

Round and About

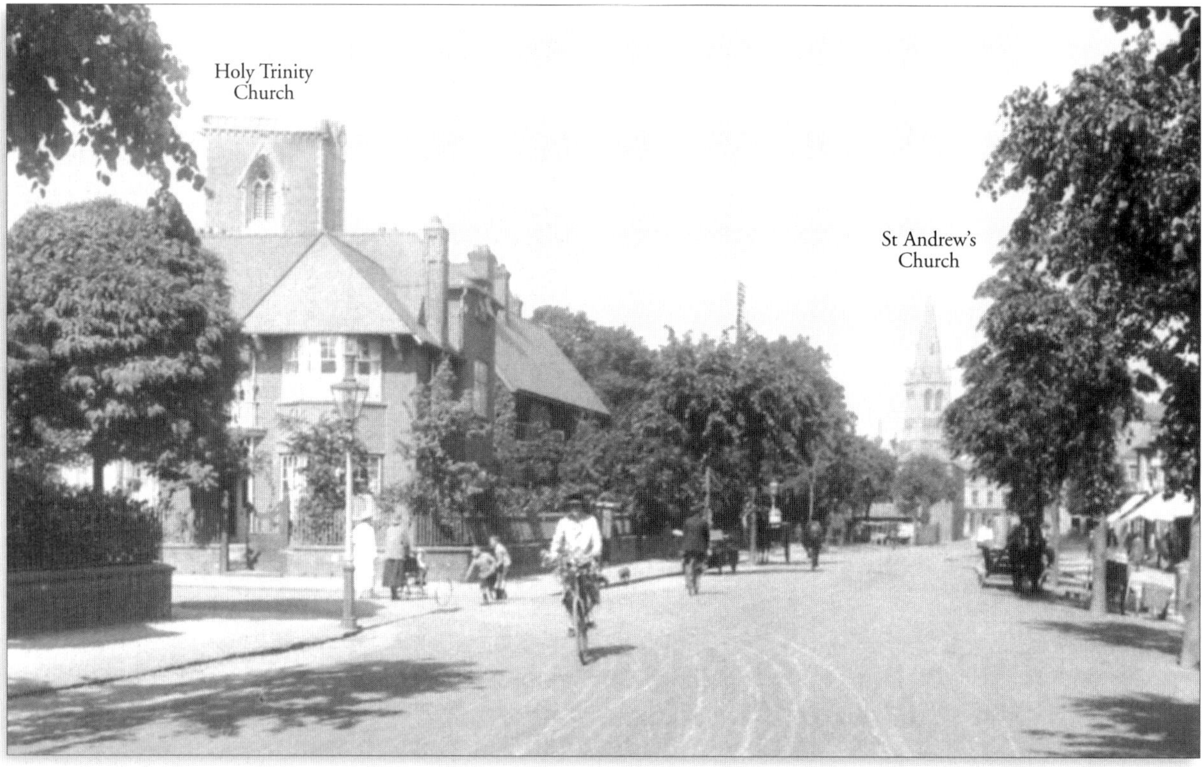

Clifton Road 1922 72122

Vandals had defeated two previous attempts to plant the Jubilee trees, but in 1886 money for 127 new trees — and for the guards to watch over them — was raised by public subscription. To the left, out of camera shot, lies Rugby School Lower School (Lawrence Sheriff School). The shops on the right had all been private houses only a few years earlier.

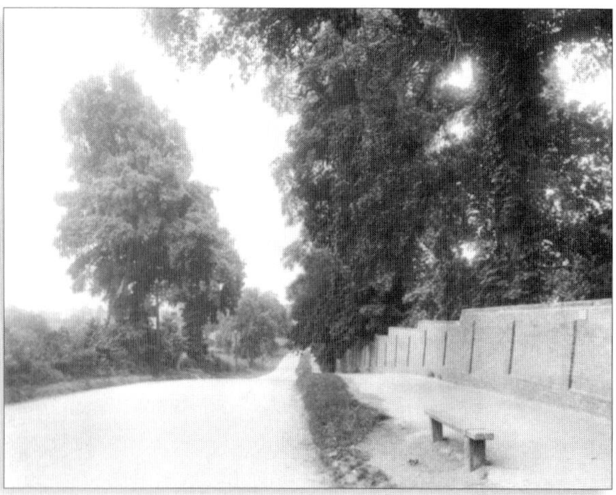

Dunchurch Road 1922 72130

Dunchurch Road, now part of the busy A426, is crossed just outside the town by a small brook. In the 18th century a young girl died after swallowing arsenic, but as a suicide her body was ordered to be buried at a cross-roads. Since there was no cross-roads in the parish, she was buried where this brook crossed at right angles to the road.

THE WAR MEMORIAL GATES 1922 72139

In 1922, Field Marshall Earl French of Ypres, in the presence of 10,000-15,000 people, unveiled these handsome wrought-iron gates to the Whitehall Recreation Ground as a memorial to Rugby's 404 fallen heroes. In 1987, despite vigorous opposition, the gates were moved a few hundred yards to the left to make way for the access road to the new Ken Marriott Sports Centre.

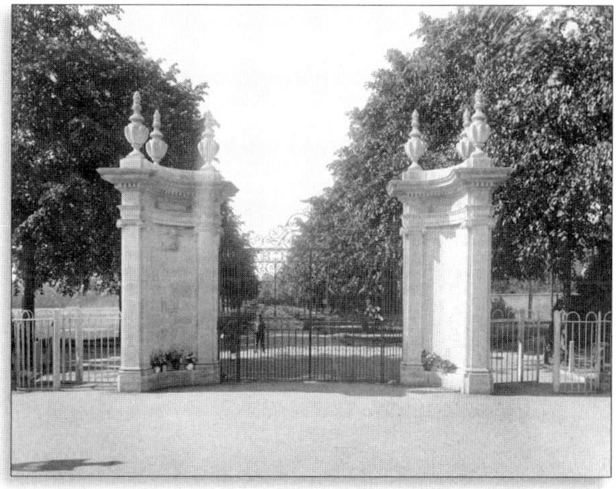

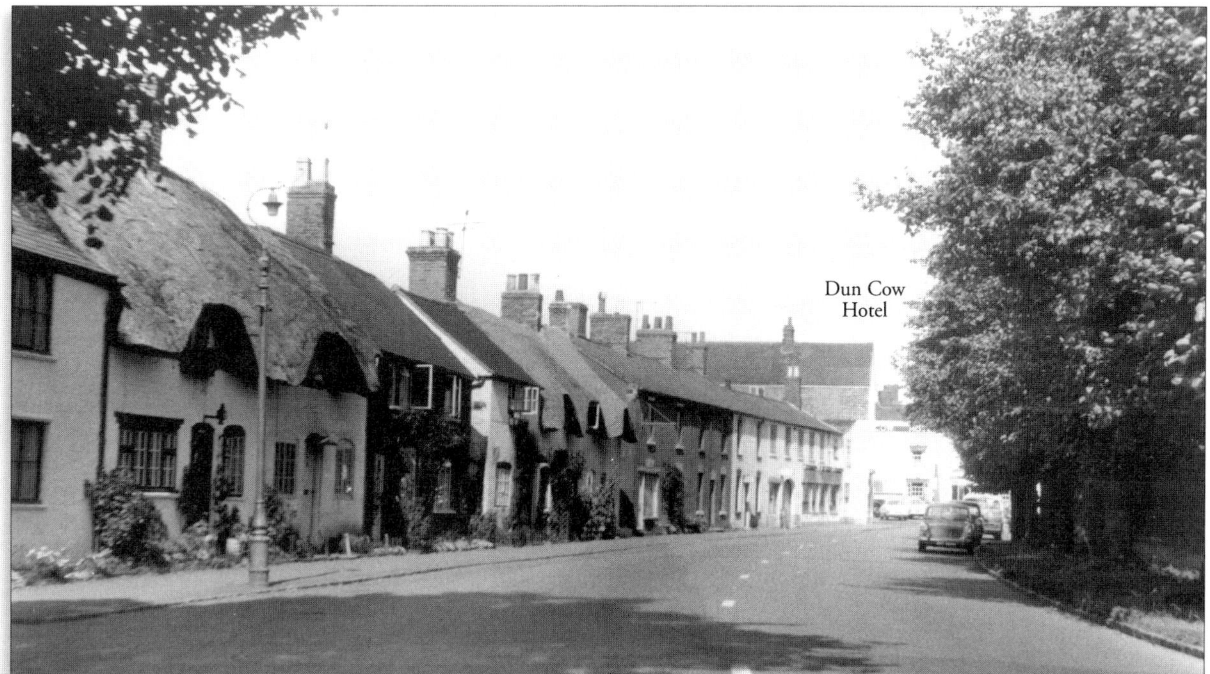

DUNCHURCH, SOUTHAM ROAD c1955 D92253

The legend of Guy of Warwick, slayer of the fearsome Dun Cow (a beast 6 yards long, 8 yards high, with eyes of red fire, immense horns and skin no blade could penetrate) is recalled in the name of the Dun Cow Hotel, a stuccoed 18th-century building with a coach entrance, just visible in this photograph beyond the row of cottages. A plaque reveals that the famous engineers, George and Robert Stephenson, dined there in 1837. The cottages have changed little since 1955, but shops now occupy those at the far end of the row, and the road is very often packed with cars.

Round and About

Until the 1880s, Dunchurch was of far greater significance than Rugby itself. This came about because, between 1707 and 1723, the installation of turnpikes on local roads led to such an improvement in their condition that Dunchurch Road became a major thoroughfare. Dunchurch itself became an important staging post on the London to Holyhead and Oxford to Leicester roads. The advent of the railways, however, brought an end both to the turnpike trusts and to Dunchurch's supremacy.

On the left of D92001, below, we can glimpse the 14th-century church of St Peter with its 15th-century tower and modern stained glass. Built of red sandstone, it is in the Perpendicular style on Saxon foundations. The Vicarage (not visible) is an attractive chequered brick Georgian house.

In The Square in front of the church there is a row of almshouses founded in 1693 by Thomas Newcombe, printer to Charles II, James II and William III. These were rebuilt in 1818. In front of the almshouses in The Square stands a statue to Lord John Douglas Montague Scott (1809-1860). Since the 1970s it has become a tradition to dress up this statue as a cartoon or TV character on New Year's Eve.

Overlooking The Square is Guy Fawkes House, a 16th-century building with vertical half-timbering and a jettied upper floor, formerly the Lion Inn. On 6 November 1605, forty Catholic gentlemen met here to dine while they awaited news of the Gunpowder Plot. When they learned of its failure, they fled, but were later captured and executed.

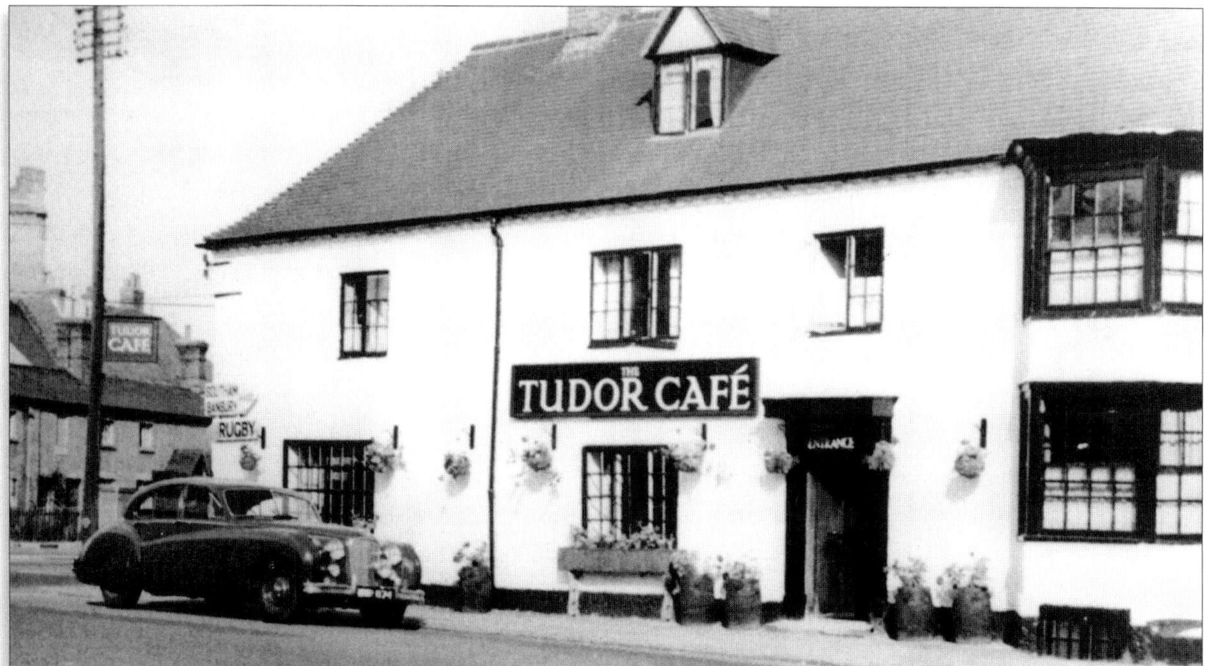

Dunchurch, The Tudor Café c1955 D92001

Originally a coaching inn, the Tudor Café became Adel's in the mid 1980s. Some 40 coaches a day passed through Dunchurch in its heyday, when there may have been as many as 27 coaching inns in the village.

TRANSPORT AND INDUSTRY

IN 1769 an Act of Parliament enabled the building of the Oxford Canal to carry coal from the mines situated at the north and north-east of Coventry to Oxford. Work on the canal, which was to encircle Rugby, was started by James Brindley in 1769 and after Brindley's death in 1772 was continued by Samuel Simcock. When the canal was completed in 1790, the price of coal in Oxford fell by 50%.

By 1773 the canal had reached the Hillmorton and Newbold area, where a flight of three locks was constructed in 1773. The men who built the navigations, the 'navvies', were forced to buy their provisions from the 'tommy shop', which was operated at excessive profit by their employer. The food was of poor quality, often rotten, and became known as 'tommy rot'. On pay-day, these navvies would terrorise the neighbourhood, including Rugby, with drunkenness and debauchery. Navvies were also employed on the railways, and Rugby would have to endure these railway navvies for many years to come.

In 1857, Robert Stephenson, engineer of the London & Birmingham Railway, wrote: 'Few people have any notion how completely the whole system of our railways has been influenced by the bend northwards at Rugby'. When Stephenson chose to take his railway north of Rugby (perhaps influenced by Rugby School's opposition to the southern route), the enforced sharp bend westwards towards Birmingham created a springboard for further lines to the north, turning Rugby into a major railway junction. Dr Arnold said of the railway: 'I rejoice to see it and to think that feudality is gone for ever'; and Matthew Bloxham commented that the railway brought 'a perceptible increase of boys at the school'.

Attracted by Rugby's excellent railway facilities, its position at the heart of the country, its cheap land and its proximity to coalfields and waterways, big manufacturing companies started to move into the town, bringing jobs and prosperity. Willans & Robinson Ltd (later GEC, now Alstom) built a factory in Rugby in 1895, its ornate architecture influenced by that of Rugby School.

In 1902 the British Thomson-Houston Company Ltd opened its 'Mazda' Lamp Factory on land beside the railway station (85195, left). Many new ideas in electric lighting were pioneered there, and for many years the streets of Rugby were used for experiments in street lighting. This factory was also a manufacturing centre for steam turbines, motors, domestic appliances and transformers.

As the town prospered, housing developments sprang up to meet the needs of the rapidly expanding population. By 1851 there were 6,851 people living in the town; the population rose to nearly 17,000 by 1901, a fifth of this being railway workers and their families. Other major employers included Rugby Cement, now one of the largest cement producers in the UK, Thomas Hunter & Co and the GPO, who in 1925 erected 12 radio masts at the Imperial Radio Station, Hillmorton (85196). Rugby's radio masts, recently reduced to just 4, are a well-known local landmark, and are visible from many directions as you approach the town.

The first transmitter sent messages for ships at sea and transmitted time signals sent via land line from Greenwich. Today, the station transmits a precision time signal from an atomic clock.

TRANSPORT AND INDUSTRY

The second transmitter, opened in 1927, provided the first public telephone service to the USA, and was the forerunner of international communications. In 1928, Edward, the Prince of Wales, was motoring past Rugby with his brother, the Duke of Gloucester, when he saw the masts and decided to pay the station a surprise visit, even ascending one of the masts in a lift.

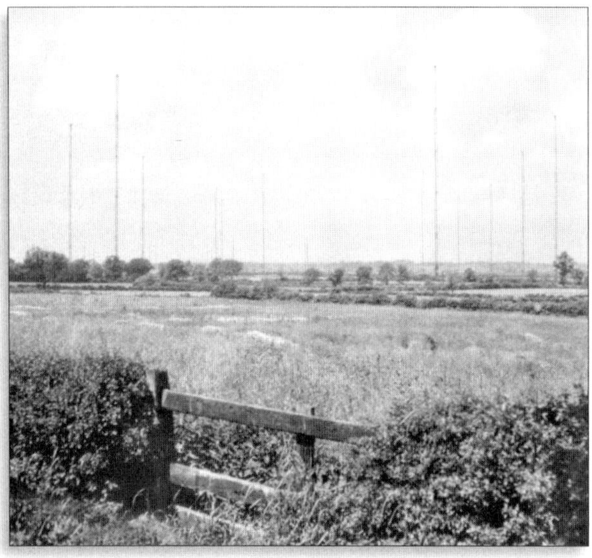

THE RADIO STATION 1932 85196

This high-powered, very low frequency telegraph transmitter is capable of world-wide range. Erection of the masts commenced in 1924 on a site chosen by the Air Ministry and the War Office. Exceptionally wet and stormy weather hindered the work, but the station was in operation by 1925, using generators supplied by British Thomson-Houston. The 12 insulated masts, each sited a quarter of a mile apart, stood 820 feet high; between them using 3,000 miles of wire.

THE RAILWAY SIDINGS 1932 85195

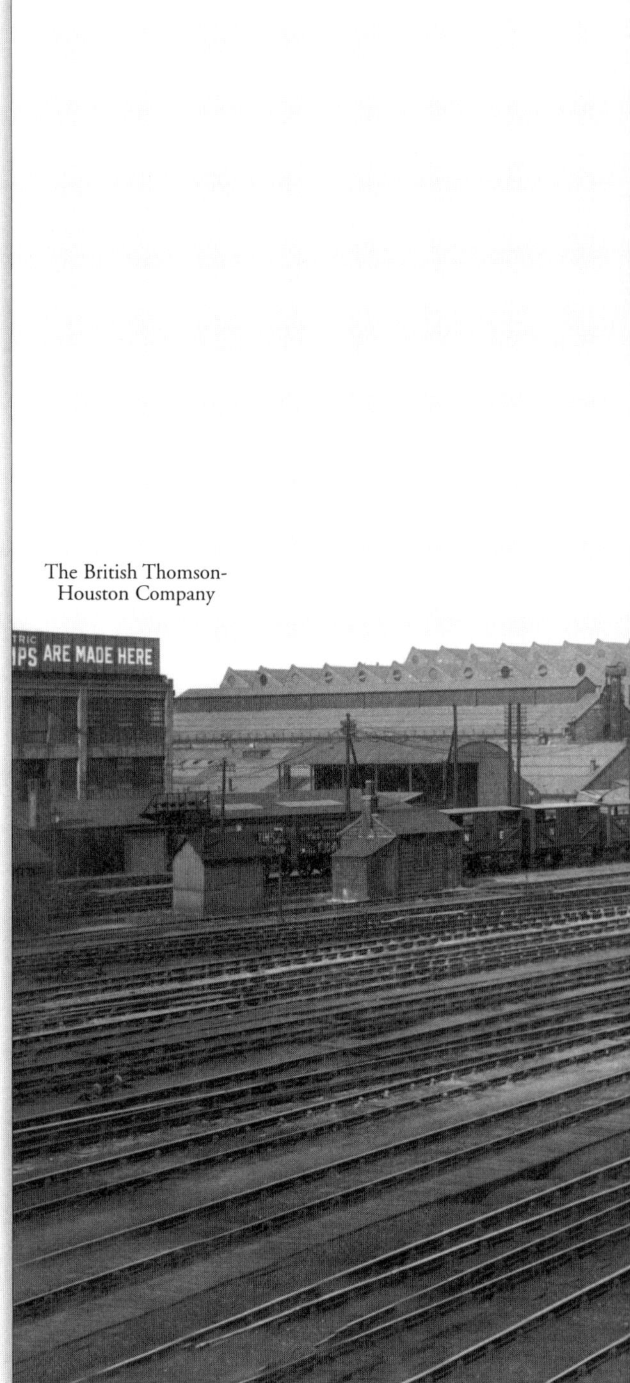

The London & Birmingham Railway opened in Rugby in 1838. The first station, off Newbold Road, was replaced in 1840 by a second station at the bottom of Station (now Railway) Terrace, intended to serve the Midland Counties Line. The Trent Valley Line opened in 1847, the Stamford Line in 1850 and the Leamington Line in 1851, by which time 60 trains a day were passing through Rugby station. In 1881 the 'New Line' opened, when a third station (built in 1886, 100 yards to the east) was required to cope with all six lines now converging on Rugby. The Great Central Line followed in 1898, but it had its own station and did not connect with the others. Its building necessitated the construction of a new 44-arm signal gantry on the London & North Western Railway. This, known as the 'bedstead and birdcage', was built in 1896, and was one of the largest in the world. It was replaced in 1939 by electric colour signalling. Of Rugby's nine lines in 1900, five were closed by 1969, leaving two lines to London and those to Birmingham and Crewe. Rugby, however, is now part of a direct link to Europe, and the station is due to undergo a major facelift.

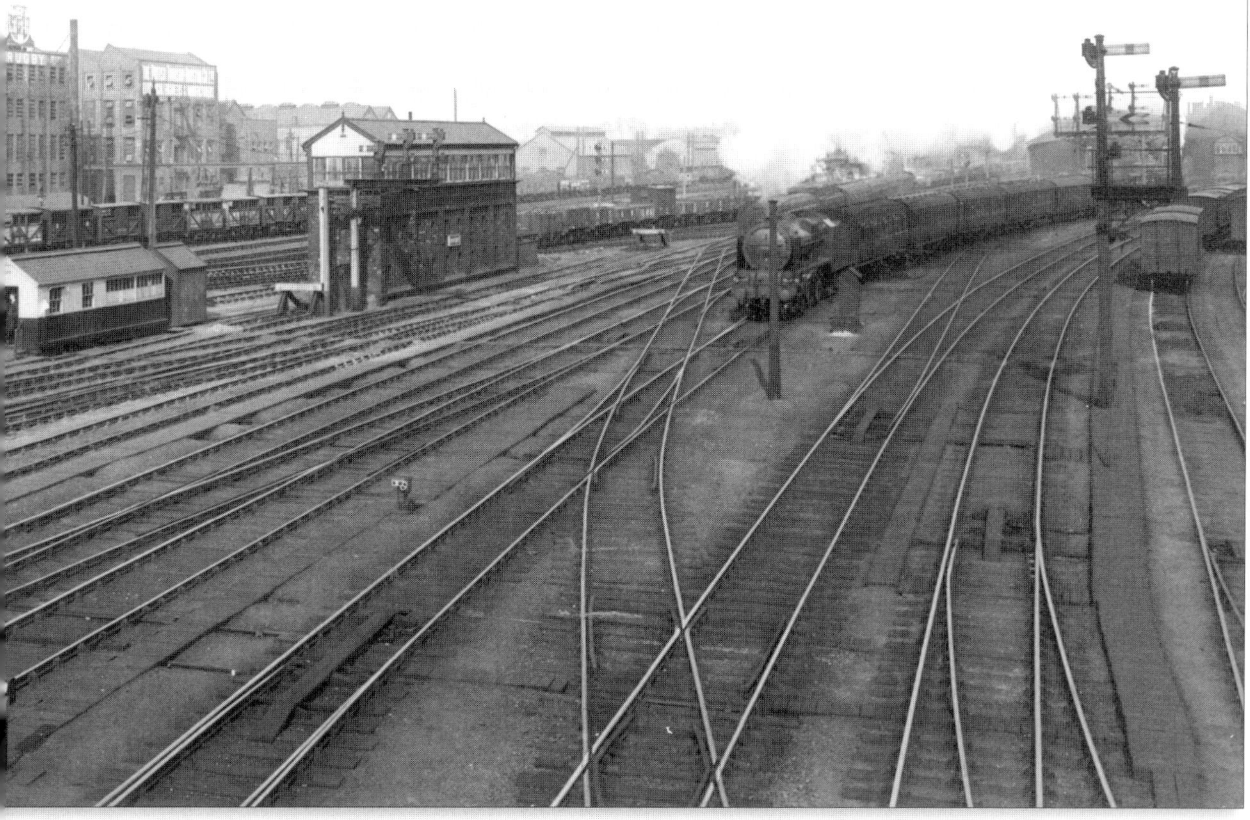

Names of Subscribers

The following people have kindly supported this book by purchasing limited edition copies prior to publication.

The Badger and Freeman families, Rugby
A tribute to the life of Ron Barton
Revd D and Mr R Bayford, Pailton, Rugby
For our parents, Frank and Eileen Bird
The Bowes Family, Rugby. In Barry's memory.
Norah Elizabeth Bradley
Chris Brain, I love you, Erica x
The Carter family, Lutterworth
To Claire on your birthday, love Mum and Dad
Brenda and Deryk Clarke, Hillmorton
Memories of Tom & Olive Clarke, Newbold
To Chris and Norman Cleaton
For George and Dora Colledge
Mich, Mary and Tim Cray, Rugby, Warwickshire
The Cunniffe Family
In memory of Edith and Charles Dandridge
To David on your birthday, love Mum and Dad
The Dean Family, in memory of David Dean
Barbara Dougherty
Maurice Dougherty
A W and V L Drake, Rugby
Peter Dunkley, Rugby
Divya and Richard Elcocks
For our Dad, Richard Fairbrother
Gerald and Sheila Fry, Lutterworth, 2006
Mark and Flick Furber, Rugby
Alan and Val Gammidge
Deanna & Graham Gare and family, Rugby
The Gordon Family, Newbold, Rugby
The Graham Family, Rugby
C and A, Donna, Kelly, Baz, Nan Witch and Pappy Grout
Jaz, Ray, Lilly, Robin, Warwick and Teigan
S G Hall
Patricia Mary Hammond
Sidney Harris
The Hart Family, Rugby 2006
Arthur and Jean Hart (née Robotham)
In memory of Robert and Margaret Hawkins
The Howells Family, in memory of Cassie
Peter Iredale
My lovely Goddaughter Jessica
Muriel Johnson
Margaret and Clive Jones of Rugby
For Leanda and Adam, from Mum and Dad xx
Derek John Leeson
Mr and Mrs J Lenton, Rugby
The Lorden Family, Rugby
Marjorie Martin
Nick Miller, for his birthday, love Mum and Dad
The Miller Family, Rugby
The Mills Family, Dunchurch
Robin and Cynthia Mold, Rugby
To John Moore, a lifelong Rugbeian
In memory of Olive (Mum), from Dody
John O'Rourke
Jane and Ted Pallot 2006
Peter, Tracey, Adam & Ben, Rugby 2005
Jim Porter
The Proudfoot family, Rugby
Peter, Julie, Stephanie and Nicola Reilly
In memory of Ethel May Renard née Herbert, Rugby
Norma Roberts
Diane and Peter Roberts
Mr & Mrs R L Roberts and Caroline, Rugby
Sarah Roberts and Kyle Skidmore, Rugby
Anne Rogers
In memory of Ted Russell, my husband. Joy.
Richard and Carol Sage
Sean Salisbury
Rebecca Salisbury
Susan Sargent, Rugby
Brian Shilvock and son Christopher
Richard Stocking
Raymond H Townsend
The Tweddle family, Rugby
In memory of Harry and Mary Wakelin, from Josie
Ray and Doreen Walker
Albert G Wells, Coventry
Philip Wenlock, Happy Birthday, 2006
Graham Wenlock, Happy Birthday, 2006
Linda and David Wilson, on their Pearl Wedding
To Granny, Zoë Constance Windsor (née Howes)
Delia M Wood and family

Index

The Francis Frith Collection Titles

www.francisfrith.com

The Francis Frith Collection publishes over 100 new titles each year. A selection of those currently available is listed below. For latest catalogue please contact The Francis Frith Collection. ***Town Books*** 96 pages, approximately 75 photos. ***County and Themed Books*** 128 pages, approximately 135 photos (unless specified). Pocket Albums are miniature editions of Frith local history books 128 pages, approximately 95 photos.

Accrington Old and New
Alderley Edge and Wilmslow
Amersham, Chesham and Rickmansworth
Andover
Around Abergavenny
Around Alton
Aylesbury
Barnstaple
Bedford
Bedfordshire
Berkshire Living Memories
Berkshire Pocket Album
Blackpool Pocket Album
Bognor Regis
Bournemouth
Bradford
Bridgend
Bridport
Brighton and Hove
Bristol
Buckinghamshire
Calne Living Memories
Camberley Pocket Album
Canterbury Cathedral
Cardiff Old and New
Chatham and the Medway Towns
Chelmsford
Chepstow Then and Now
Cheshire
Cheshire Living Memories
Chester
Chesterfield
Chigwell
Christchurch
Churches of East Cornwall
Clevedon
Clitheroe
Corby Living Memories
Cornish Coast
Cornwall Living Memories
Cotswold Living Memories
Cotswold Pocket Album
Coulsdon, Chipstead and Woodmanstern
County Durham
Cromer, Sheringham and Holt
Dartmoor Pocket Album
Derby
Derbyshire
Derbyshire Living Memories
Devon
Devon Churches
Dorchester
Dorset Coast Pocket Album
Dorset Living Memories
Dorset Villages
Down the Dart
Down the Severn
Down the Thames
Dunmow, Thaxted and Finchingfield
Durham
East Anglia Pocket Album
East Devon
East Grinstead
Edinburgh
Ely and The Fens
Essex Pocket Album
Essex Second Selection
Essex: The London Boroughs
Exeter
Exmoor
Falmouth
Farnborough, Fleet and Aldershot
Folkestone
Frome
Furness and Cartmel Peninsulas
Glamorgan
Glasgow
Glastonbury
Gloucester
Gloucestershire
Greater Manchester
Guildford
Hailsham
Hampshire
Harrogate
Hastings and Bexhill
Haywards Heath Living Memories
Heads of the Valleys
Heart of Lancashire Pocket Album
Helston
Herefordshire
Horsham
Humberside Pocket Album
Huntingdon, St Neots and St Ives
Hythe, Romney Marsh and Ashford
Ilfracombe
Ipswich Pocket Album
Isle of Wight
Isle of Wight Living Memories
King's Lynn
Kingston upon Thames
Lake District Pocket Album
Lancashire Living Memories
Lancashire Villages

Available from your local bookshop or from the publisher

The Francis Frith Collection Titles (continued)

Lancaster, Morecambe and Heysham Pocket Album
Leeds Pocket Album
Leicester
Leicestershire
Lincolnshire Living Memoires
Lincolnshire Pocket Album
Liverpool and Merseyside
London Pocket Album
Ludlow
Maidenhead
Maidstone
Malmesbury
Manchester Pocket Album
Marlborough
Matlock
Merseyside Living Memories
Nantwich and Crewe
New Forest
Newbury Living Memories
Newquay to St Ives
North Devon Living Memories
North London
North Wales
North Yorkshire
Northamptonshire
Northumberland
Northwich
Nottingham
Nottinghamshire Pocket Album
Oakham
Odiham Then and Now
Oxford Pocket Album
Oxfordshire
Padstow
Pembrokeshire
Penzance
Petersfield Then and Now
Plymouth
Poole and Sandbanks
Preston Pocket Album
Ramsgate Old and New
Reading Pocket Album
Redditch Living Memories
Redhill to Reigate
Richmond
Ringwood
Rochdale
Romford Pocket Album
Salisbury Pocket Album
Scotland
Scottish Castles
Sevenoaks and Tonbridge
Sheffield and South Yorkshire Pocket Album
Shropshire
Somerset
South Devon Coast
South Devon Living Memories
South East London
Southampton Pocket Album
Southend Pocket Album
Southport
Southwold to Aldeburgh
Stourbridge Living Memories
Stratford upon Avon
Stroud
Suffolk
Suffolk Pocket Album
Surrey Living Memories
Sussex
Sutton
Swanage and Purbeck
Swansea Pocket Album
Swindon Living Memories
Taunton
Teignmouth
Tenby and Saundersfoot
Tiverton
Torbay
Truro
Uppingham
Villages of Kent
Villages of Surrey
Villages of Sussex Pocket Album
Wakefield and the Five Towns Living Memories
Warrington
Warwick
Warwickshire Pocket Album
Wellingborough Living Memories
Wells
Welsh Castles
West Midlands Pocket Album
West Wiltshire Towns
West Yorkshire
Weston-super-Mare
Weymouth
Widnes and Runcorn
Wiltshire Churches
Wiltshire Living Memories
Wiltshire Pocket Album
Wimborne
Winchester Pocket Album
Windermere
Windsor
Wirral
Wokingham and Bracknell
Woodbridge
Worcester
Worcestershire
Worcestershire Living Memories
Wyre Forest
York Pocket Album
Yorkshire
Yorkshire Coastal Memories
Yorkshire Dales
Yorkshire Revisited

Frith Products & Services

Francis Frith would doubtless be pleased to know that the pioneering publishing venture he started in 1860 still continues today. Over a hundred and forty years later, The Francis Frith Collection continues in the same innovative tradition and is now one of the foremost publishers of vintage photographs in the world. Some of the current activities include:

Interior Decoration

Today Frith's photographs can be seen framed and as giant wall murals in thousands of pubs, restaurants, hotels, banks, retail stores and other public buildings throughout the country. In every case they enhance the unique local atmosphere of the places they depict and provide reminders of gentler days in an increasingly busy and frenetic world.

Product Promotions

Frith products are used by many major companies to promote the sales of their own products or to reinforce their own history and heritage. Frith promotions have been used by Hovis bread, Courage beers, Scots Porage Oats, Colman's mustard, Cadbury's foods, Mellow Birds coffee, Dunhill pipe tobacco, Guinness, and Bulmer's Cider.

Genealogy and Family History

As the interest in family history and roots grows world-wide, more and more people are turning to Frith's photographs of Great Britain for images of the towns, villages and streets where their ancestors lived; and, of course, photographs of the churches and chapels where their ancestors were christened, married and buried are an essential part of every genealogy tree and family album.

Frith Products

All Frith photographs are available Framed or just as Mounted Prints and Posters (size 23 x 16 inches). These may be ordered from the address below. From time to time other products - Address Books, Calendars, Table Mats, etc - are available.

The Internet

Already ninety thousand Frith photographs can be viewed and purchased on the internet through the Frith websites and a myriad of partner sites.

For more detailed information on Frith companies and products, look at this site:

www.francisfrith.com

See the complete list of Frith Books at:

www.francisfrith.com

This web site is regularly updated with the latest list of publications from The Francis Frith Collection. If you wish to buy books relating to another part of the country that your local bookshop does not stock, you may purchase on-line.

For further information, trade, or author enquiries please contact us at the address below:

The Francis Frith Collection, Frith's Barn, Teffont, Salisbury, Wiltshire, England SP3 5QP.

Tel: +44 (0)1722 716 376 Fax: +44 (0)1722 716 881 Email: sales@francisfrith.co.uk

See Frith books on the internet at www.francisfrith.com

FREE PRINT OF YOUR CHOICE

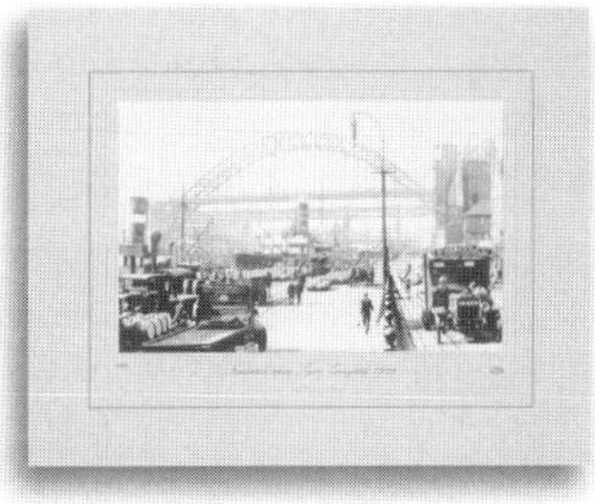

Mounted Print
Overall size 14 x 11 inches (355 x 280mm)

Choose any Frith photograph in this book. Simply complete the Voucher opposite and return it with your remittance for £3.50 (to cover postage and handling) and we will print the photograph of your choice in SEPIA (size 11 x 8 inches) and supply it in a cream mount with a burgundy rule line (overall size 14 x 11 inches). **Please note: photographs with a reference number starting with a "Z" are not Frith photographs and cannot be supplied under this offer.**
Offer valid for delivery to one UK address only.

***PLUS:* Order additional Mounted Prints at HALF PRICE - £7.49 each** (normally £14.99)
If you would like to order more Frith prints from this book, possibly as gifts for friends and family, you can buy them at half price (with no additional postage and handling costs).

***PLUS:* Have your Mounted Prints framed**
For an extra £14.95 per print you can have your mounted print(s) framed in an elegant polished wood and gilt moulding, overall size 16 x 13 inches (no additional postage and handling required).

IMPORTANT!

These special prices are only available if you use this form to order. You must use the ORIGINAL VOUCHER on this page (no copies permitted). We can only despatch to one UK address. This offer cannot be combined with any other offer.

Send completed Voucher form to:
The Francis Frith Collection, Frith's Barn, Teffont, Salisbury, Wiltshire SP3 5QP

CHOOSE A PHOTOGRAPH FROM THIS BOOK

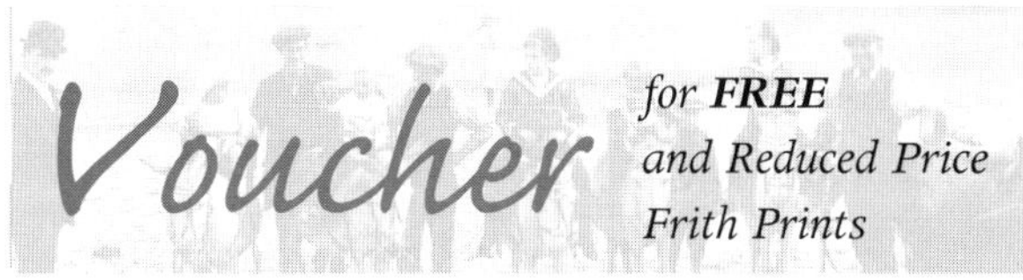

Please do not photocopy this voucher. Only the original is valid, so please fill it in, cut it out and return it to us with your order.

Picture ref no	Page no	Qty	Mounted @ £7.49	Framed + £14.95	Total Cost £
		1	Free of charge*	£	£
			£7.49	£	£
			£7.49	£	£
			£7.49	£	£
			£7.49	£	£
			£7.49	£	£
Please allow 28 days for delivery.			* Post & handling		£3.50
Offer available to one UK address only			Total Order Cost		£

Title of this book ....
I enclose a cheque/postal order for £ ....
made payable to 'The Francis Frith Collection'

OR please debit my Mastercard / Visa / Maestro card, details below

Card Number

Issue No (Maestro only) Valid from (Maestro)

Expires Signature

Name Mr/Mrs/Ms ....
Address ....
....
....
.... Postcode ....
Daytime Tel No ....
Email ....

ISBN 1-85937-620-7 Valid to 31/12/09

Free Print - see overleaf

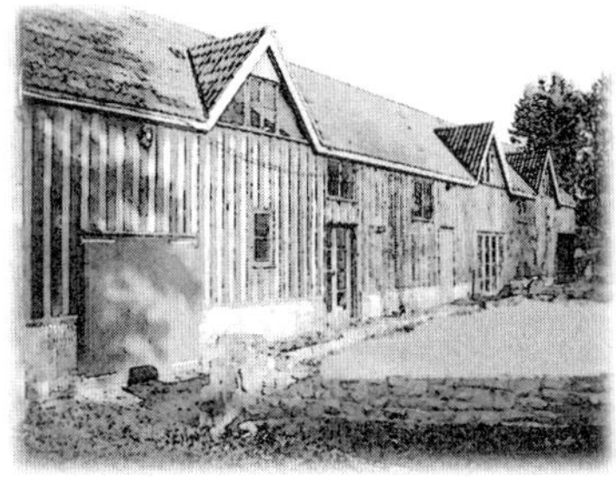

Can you help us with information about any of the Frith photographs in this book?

We are gradually compiling an historical record for each of the photographs in the Frith archive. It is always fascinating to find out the names of the people shown in the pictures, as well as insights into the shops, buildings and other features depicted.

If you recognize anyone in the photographs in this book, or if you have information not already included in the author's caption, do let us know. We would love to hear from you, and will try to publish it in future books or articles.

Our production team

Frith books are produced by a small dedicated team at offices in the converted Grade II listed 18th-century barn at Teffont near Salisbury, illustrated above. Most have worked with The Francis Frith Collection for many years. All have in common one quality: they have a passion for The Francis Frith Collection. The team is constantly expanding, but currently includes:

Andrew Alsop, Paul Baron, Jason Buck, John Buck, Jenny Coles, Heather Crisp, David Davies, Natalie Davis, Louis du Mont, Isobel Hall, Chris Hardwick, Neil Harvey, Julian Hight, Peter Horne, James Kinnear, Karen Kinnear, Tina Leary, Stuart Login, Sue Molloy, Sarah Roberts, Kate Rotondetto, Eliza Sackett, Terence Sackett, Sandra Sampson, Adrian Sanders, Sandra Sanger, Julia Skinner, Lewis Taylor, Will Tunnicliffe, David Turner and Ricky Williams.